TEACH YO

LAPIDARY

Lapidary is the art and craft of working gem stones, taking rough, jagged fragments of rock and smoothing and polishing them to produce beautiful, shapely stones. It is an absorbing and satisfying hobby and is fast growing in popularity.

In this general introduction to lapidary, the basic processes of cutting, grinding, sanding and polishing gem stones are explained step by step and the more advanced techniques of drilling, lapping and facetting discussed. The equipment each process requires is described and illustrated, and the reader is shown how to make many of the necessary tools and machines himself. There is a valuable chapter listing the gem stones commonly available, with notes on their appearance, hardness and special requirements, and the author has also included a brief account of jewellery-making. Among the useful information given in the appendices at the end of the book are lists of lapidary supply houses, clubs and societies throughout the country.

TEACH YOURSELF BOOKS

LAPIDARY

Del Fairfield

TEACH YOURSELF BOOKS
HODDER & STOUGHTON

ST. PAUL'S HOUSE   WARWICK LANE
LONDON EC4P 4AH

First printed 1973
Third impression 1975

ISBN 0 340 18254 7

*Printed in Great Britain for Teach Yourself Books, Hodder & Stoughton
by Fletcher & Son Ltd, Norwich, and bound by
Richard Clay (The Chaucer Press) Ltd, Bungay, Suffolk*

Contents

1	Lapidary, What Is It?	7
2	The Tumble Polisher	11
3	Diamond Saws	22
4	Grinding Machines	37
5	Sanding and Polishing	53
6	Combination Machines	67
7	Lapping	71
8	Drilling	78
9	Facetting	86
10	Gem Materials	96
11	Setting Up a Workshop	108
12	Making Jewellery	113
	Appendices	117

1 Lapidary, What Is It?

It is only fitting that a splendid pursuit should have a splendid name. Lapidary originally meant a worker in stone – generally building stone – but was later restricted to the worker in gem stones. Somehow, over the centuries, the word has expanded to describe the art of working gem stones and also the place where such an art is carried out. A lapidary practises lapidary in a lapidary!

As if this isn't enough, the professional lapidaries seem determined to call themselves something else. They have adopted the titles of 'diamond cutter', 'diamond polisher', and, if they work with any other gem stones, appear to be rather contemptuously dismissed as 'coloured stone workers'. So in this particular example of the evolution of language, lapidary is a craft practised mostly by amateurs.

Observant readers will have noticed that I have added to the confusion by referring to lapidary as an art and later as a craft. It has to be both. Many of the processes of cutting and polishing gem stones require a little skill which is soon acquired. Other processes require, in addition, an awareness and understanding of colour and form which make it an art.

But what is a gem stone? Most people when asked would respond by listing those gem stones they can remember and letting that suffice. It doesn't really answer the question. In its widest sense, a gem stone is that which is decorative and sufficiently hard to withstand the knocks and rubbings to which any piece of jewellery is subjected.

Definitions have a tricky habit of posing another question,

and now we are faced with 'what is sufficiently hard?'

Many people have only the haziest concept of the comparative hardness of substances. They believe, for instance, that only a diamond will cut glass. If you believe it, then try this. Pick a smooth pebble from your garden and stroke its smoothest curve upon a piece of glass (preferably not your picture window). Almost certainly it will leave a crisply cut line. Most pebbles are much harder than glass.

Many scales have been created to show the relative hardness of substances and the one used by lapidaries, minerologists and gemmologists is the Mohs Scale of Hardness. Herr Mohs introduced a scale which lists, in descending order, ten minerals such that each will scratch all the substances below them but will have no effect on those above them.

Mohs scale of hardness

10	Diamond
9	Sapphire
8	Topaz
7	Quartz
6	Orthoclase
5	Apatite
4	Fluorite
3	Calcite
2	Gypsum
1	Talc

This is not a linear scale; in fact, the difference of hardness between diamond (10) and sapphire (9) is greater than the difference between sapphire (9) and talc (1).

If glass were placed in this scale, it would appear somewhere between apatite (5) and orthoclase (6), and so all the minerals of hardness 6 or better will cut glass.

Now, perhaps, we can return to the question 'what is sufficiently hard?' Rings get the roughest treatment, so that stones which are going to be used in rings should be hardness 7 or better. Pendants, brooches and ear-rings are much more kindly used, and stones of hardness 4 or better can be employed in these applications.

Fortunately for the amateur lapidary there is a prolific group of gem materials in the quartz family (hardness 7). Besides the transparent crystals in various colours (clear, pink, yellow, brown and purple) there are the translucent chalcedonies and agates and the opaque jaspers. From this extensive group, material can be selected for any purpose and within any price range. It is probable that more quartz is handled by lapidaries than all other gem materials combined.

Logically, that which cuts must be harder than that which is cut and consequently we must find something that will cut quartz (hardness 7). The Mohs scale lists three minerals that will cut quartz and there are several others. Diamond, sapphire, spinel, ruby, emerald, aquamarine, topaz and garnet will all cut quartz, and until the twentieth century a lapidary would use one or other of these stones, crushed into powder, in order to abrade and polish an amethyst or citrine (the purple and yellow forms of quartz).

The discovery of silicon carbide (SiC) has changed all that. Silicon carbide, which is harder than any mineral except diamond, is cheap to manufacture and readily available. It is made by baking together in an electric furnace two very mundane materials, clay and coke. The resultant compound is crushed and graded and, in one form or another, makes modern lapidary possible. It is used as loose powder, compressed into grinding wheels or bonded to paper and cloth.

The method of grading silicon carbide is worth an

explanation. Imagine a fine mesh which has 100 divisions per linear inch. A square inch of this mesh would have 100 × 100 = 10 000 holes. Silicon carbide grains that pass through this mesh are called 100 grit. The coarse grits, therefore, have the low numbers and lapidaries use a selection of grits numbered 46, 80, 100, 220, 320, 400, 600 and 1200. Prices of these grits vary according to grade and quantity purchased – the finer grades being the more costly – but they are all remarkably cheap considering their usefulness.

2 The Tumble Polisher

A tremendous number of people have become lapidaries because their children collected some pretty pebbles on the beach. When the pebbles were picked up they were wet and gleaming: the colours and patterns were crisp and clear. Unfortunately, by the time they were unpacked at home the colours had dulled and the surfaces were rough. The kids, naturally enough, were unhappy about this, so what else could their parents do except set about improving on nature.

The action of the sea on fragments of rock is a gentle rolling and tumbling one upon another, with the fine fragments, sand, scouring and smoothing. A tumble polisher can do all this and more. It can produce on the pebbles a mirror polish which only the most brutal treatment can spoil.

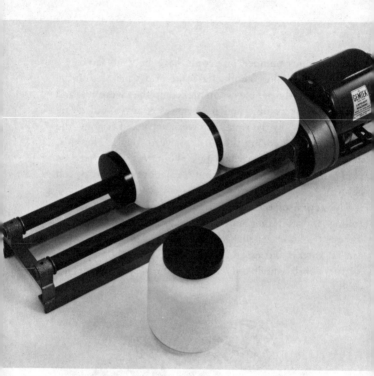

Gemtek tumbler. (*Gemstones, Hull.*)

A tumble polisher is, usually, a rotating drum which contains the pebbles or rock fragments and a grinding medium of water and silicon carbide grit. As the barrel rotates, the pebbles are tumbled over and over in contact with each other and with the silicon carbide, which gradually reduces the stones to a smooth shape and finally produces a polished surface.

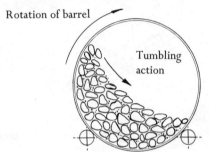

Rotation of barrel

Tumbling action

Section through tumbler barrel showing the action of stones when rotation is correct. Too slow, the stones will lie at the bottom. Too fast, centrifugal force will carry them round with no tumbling action.

The process, from rough, jagged rock fragments to smoothly polished, shapely stones, takes several weeks, which, even if it does seem a long time, is a considerable improvement on nature. To keep the period as short as possible it is necessary to have the tumbler operating twenty-four hours a day, and this introduces some problems. Tumbling is not a silent process. It is accompanied by a swishing and rumbling sound as the pebbles roll and is therefore best relegated to the garage. It is also advisable to check that the electric motor driving the tumbler is a 'continuous rating' type – that is, capable of running day and night for a considerable period without creating any great increase in temperature.

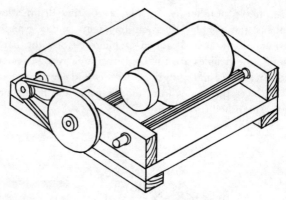

Simple tumbler using a heavy-duty polythene jar.

Perhaps a detailed description of a charge of rough rock taken right through the tumbling process will answer most questions.

Assemble the pieces of rock and, if they are of various varieties, check that they are of similar hardnesses. As a rough and ready technique, divide them into rocks harder than glass and those softer. This can be done easily by trying to scratch a piece of glass with each stone. All pieces harder than glass will happily tumble together, but those softer than glass may need further subdivisions.

Place the selected pieces into the tumbler barrel until it is about two-thirds full. Remove the stones from the barrel and weigh them. Then put them back in the barrel and add just enough water to cover the stones. Silicon carbide grit, grade 80, is now added at the rate of 1 ounce to 1 pound of stones. Fix the lid on securely and ensure that no leaks occur when the barrel is inverted and shaken vigorously. Place the barrel on the tumbler bed, switch on the power and leave the tumbler rotating for seven days.

It is advisable to take the barrel off the tumbler bed every day and momentarily loosen and retighten the lid. Some stones when tumbled create an increase in gas pressure, so this daily 'burping the barrel' is desirable as a precaution.

After seven days place a colander in a plastic bowl and empty the barrel into it. Fill the barrel with clean water, swill it around and empty it over the stones. Do not, under any circumstances, empty the silicon carbide/stone residue down the sink, since it will fall to the bottom of your drainage system and set like cement. It seems to do no harm if emptied on the garden and dug in.

Now wash the stones thoroughly, and notice how the sharp edges and corners have been eroded. Accurate before and after weighing would show about a 5 per cent reduction.

The clean stones are replaced in the clean barrel and again covered with water. One ounce of silicon carbide per pound of stone is again added, this time of 220 grade. Check the lid and recommence tumbling.

220 grit slowly loses its cutting ability over approximately ten days, but it is worth checking after a week to see if sufficient cutting has been achieved. This will, of course, depend on the hardness of the stones. If more cutting is required, then add a few ounces more of 220 grit and tumble on.

When the 220 stage is completed, rinse the stones as before and then pick them over carefully. Any that seem unworthy of finishing can be discarded and any that need further rough grinding can be put aside to await the next batch going through.

Clean the stones and barrel thoroughly, and then add 1 ounce of 400 grit per pound with sufficient water just to cover the stones and tumble them for a week or ten days. At the end of this stage the stones should be quite smooth and, when wet, should reveal all their colours and lustre. They are now ready for polishing.

It is well worth while having a second tumbler barrel which is used only for the polishing stage. If you must use the grinding barrel, then ensure that no single grain of silicon carbide grit is left in it before adding the scrupulously washed stones.

The polishing medium is not silicon carbide but a metallic oxide, usually tin oxide or cerium oxide. Try them both and decide which you prefer. Make up a thin slurry with water added to $\frac{1}{2}$ ounce of oxide per pound of stones and then pour this over the stones in the barrel.

It is customary to add a quantity of soft material to the barrel to provide cushioning during the polishing process and also to carry the polishing material. Various materials have their advocates, including leather, wood, hardboard, plastic granules, cork crumbs, etc. Leather, for instance, should be heavy soling leather cut into $\frac{1}{2}$-inch squares, and wood should be in $\frac{1}{2}$-inch cubes. This additional material should be about one-third the volume of stones, and when stones, cushions and slurry are all mixed up there should be an adequate coating over everything but not much spare slurry.

The barrel should be tumbled for three days and then a few stones removed, washed carefully and allowed to dry. If they retain their gleaming polish when dry, then the process is finished and the remainder of the stones can be removed. If the gleam fades when the stones dry, then continue the process for a few more days. Try to retain the tin oxide and cushions since they can be re-used.

The polished stones should be replaced in the cleaned polishing barrel together with plenty of water and a good squeeze of washing-up liquid. Tumble the mixture for half an hour and then wash thoroughly in lots of clear water.

No amount of polishing will give lustre to stones that need more fine grinding, so, if after a week of polishing your stones still look frosted when washed and dried, they will need to go back for another session in 400 or 600 grit.

There appears to be a fair amount of personal magic in tumbling and the process or material that works fine for your friend may well be no good at all when you try it. This is to be expected in a process that has so many variables in barrel size, rotation speed, type of stones, sizes of stones, quantities of stones, grits, water, etc. For this reason it is essential to keep a tumbling log in which as many details as possible are entered. You will then find it easier to repeat your successes and eliminate your failures.

Tumblers are available from lapidary suppliers in a bewildering range of shapes and sizes. Single-, double- and triple-barrel models can be obtained, and the capacities of the barrels vary from a handful to a bucketful. Barrels can be made of steel, of plastic, of solid rubber or of steel with rubber liners.

Barrels can be round in section, or hexagonal, octagonal or any other polygonal shape. Some tumblers are made in Britain and many others are imported from America and Australia.

Advice as to which is the best depends on so many factors. The thought of buying a big tumbler and producing masses of beautiful, polished stones is tempting, but what will you do with them all? Unless you have ideas of casting them in clear resin plastic to make coffee-table tops, there is a limit to the number of tumbled stones you can use.

Even if you finish up tumbling vast quantities of stones, there will always be times when you will want to run a small batch of specials through, so a small tumbler will always be useful. As a first purchase I would recommend a small plastic- or rubber-barrelled tumbler with a capacity of 1 or 2 pounds of stones.

Amateur-made tumblers exist in many styles and use a

variety of power sources. Car tyres hanging on a shaft rotated by a small windmill and polygonal sectional wooden barrels operated by a small water wheel are two of the more bizarre designs successfully created by amateur constructors.

Most of us depend on mains electricity for our power source and the tumblers we create are likely to be rather conventional too.

Basically, a simple tumbler consists of two parallel shafts running in bearings, one of them coupled by pulleys and belt to a small continuous-rated electric motor of about $\frac{1}{16}$ hp.

If the shafts are $\frac{1}{2}$ or $\frac{3}{4}$ inch diameter they can have lengths of suitable-sized hose-pipe pushed over them to give traction to the barrel. The shafts must run in bearings, but this is one lapidary machine where the bearings can be plain instead of ball bearings. A plain bearing is a short tube of bronze in which a shaft can rotate easily.

There is no reason, therefore, why the tumbler should not be built on a wooden framework. The two end pieces holding the bearings should be drilled together, the bearings slid into the holes with a smear of adhesive, the shafts pushed through to ensure alignment, and the two end pieces glued and pinned to a base board large enough to hold the motor as well. The distance between the bearing boards should be $\frac{1}{2}$ inch longer than the length of your barrel – or barrels. The distance between the shafts from centre to centre should be about two-thirds the diameter of the barrel.

When the bearing boards are set, the shafts should be removed and then re-inserted, pushing them through lengths of ribbed hose-pipe. Short pieces of hose-pipe should also be pushed over the projections of the shafts so that they can be coupled with a stout rubber band or a piece of

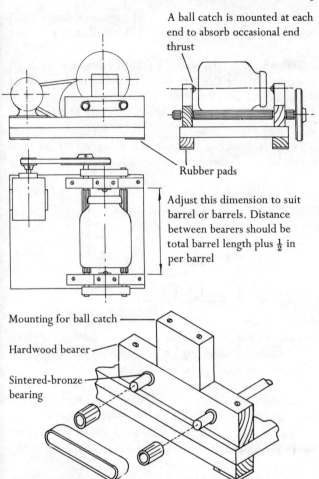

A ball catch is mounted at each end to absorb occasional end thrust

Rubber pads

Adjust this dimension to suit barrel or barrels. Distance between bearers should be total barrel length plus $\frac{1}{2}$ in per barrel

Mounting for ball catch

Hardwood bearer

Sintered-bronze bearing

After assembly, glue short lengths of hose pipe onto the projecting rods and slip on one or two bands of inner tube to transfer drive to the idler rod. Note that the driven rod must be longer to accept the pulley.

inner tube. This ensures that, although only one shaft is directly coupled to the motor, both shafts will turn together.

The pulleys on the motor and shaft must be selected so as to ensure that the barrel rotates at the correct speed; other factors to be considered are motor speed, shaft diameter and barrel diameter. An example of this calculation may suffice.

Let us suppose that your barrel is going to be a $\frac{1}{2}$-gallon, heavy-duty, polythene screw-top jar, which is made for

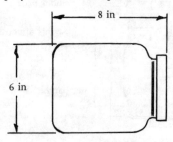

this purpose and sold by many of the lapidary stockists. We will also suppose that the shafts are $\frac{1}{2}$ inch diameter covered with standard-quality garden hose-pipe, the outside diameter of which is approximately $\frac{5}{8}$ inch.

We require a barrel rotation of about 35 revolutions per minute and, because of their relative diameters, the shafts must rotate at ten times that speed, i.e. 350 r.p.m. The motor speed (standard) is 1420 r.p.m., so that we now need a reduction between motor and shaft of approximately 4 to 1.

The small pulley ($1\frac{1}{2}$-in dia.) will go on the motor and the large (6-in dia.) pulley on the driven shaft. Since this is a gentle operation, the pulley and belt can be of a light-duty, V-belt type. (See the appendices for a list of manufacturers and suppliers of these and other items.)

Barrel speeds will depend on barrel sizes, and if you use a barrel other than the one used in the calculation you will need to substitute other figures. The larger the barrel, the slower it must rotate, and vice versa. An 8-inch diameter barrel should rotate at about 25 r.p.m. and a 4-inch barrel at about 45 r.p.m.

If you are making your own tumbler you can easily incorporate a refinement which few commercial manufacturers bother with. When you come to the polishing stage it is a very good thing to reduce the speed by a few revs. This can be done by slotting the holes in the board on which the motor is mounted so that adjustments can be made and then fitting a larger pulley to the tumbler shaft (or a smaller pulley on the motor shaft). In the example given, a substitution of a $1\frac{1}{4}$-inch pulley for the $1\frac{1}{2}$-inch pulley would give a gear reduction of about 6 r.p.m., or a 7-inch pulley instead of a 6-inch pulley would give a similar reduction.

This sort of reduction is of great value in polishing. It would obviously do no harm to have this speed for all stages of tumbling, but it would add several days to the overall time taken.

Always ensure that the bearings are lubricated. A few drops of fairly heavy oil on every bearing once a week should ensure a long, useful life. Remember, however, that a grain or two of silicon carbide grit can ruin any bearing, so wipe your barrel carefully after adding any grits.

3 Diamond Saws

Although most lapidaries start off with a tumbler, many soon become dissatisfied with the irregular 'Baroque' shapes that a tumbler produces. They feel a need to produce regular shapes cut precisely from a piece of gem material, and it then becomes necessary to increase the range of equipment.

To reduce a chunk of gem material to usable pieces in an economic fashion it is essential to use one or more diamond saws, which can slice smoothly and easily through any stone.

A diamond saw is a thin disc of steel into the rim of which is set crushed diamond grit and which is operated in a machine that is basically similar to a woodworker's circular saw. The blade may be of two types, the 'notched' blade or the 'sintered-segment' blade.

The notched blade, which is quite inexpensive, is lightly chiselled around the edge and then rolled in diamond grit or 'bort'. The notches are then hammered lightly to trap the bort and the rim is heated to combine the diamond with the metal of the blade.

The sintered-segment blade is much more costly but is probably more economical in use. Diamond grit is mixed with powdered metal and fused under heat and pressure into small blocks in a process called 'sintering'. These blocks are then soldered into recesses cut into a steel disc.

Section of sintered-segment blade showing how sintered blocks are located on the rim of the blade.

The sintered blocks are thicker than the steel disc and so they provide clearance as the saw advances into the stone.

Prices are difficult to quote in these inflationary days, but at the time of writing the price of a 6-inch notched blade is £2.50 and the price of a 6-inch diameter sintered blade is £7.00. The latter will, however, last very much longer than the cheaper blade and could be considered better value.

Diamond saws fall into two main types: the 'slabbing' saw, which is used to reduce a large chunk of stone to usable slices, and the 'trimming' saw, which cuts the slices into smaller pieces and then trims the pieces to shape preparatory to grinding and polishing. Generally, slabbing saws use blades of 10 inches diameter and up, whereas trimming saws use 4-inch to 8-inch diameter blades.

Because of the friction heat that is generated as a diamond saw cuts through gem material, it is necessary to provide a coolant liquid on the cutting edge to disperse the heat and prevent damage, either to the blade or to the stone. This necessity tends to govern the design of the saw. The majority of trimming saws and many slabbing saws have a coolant reservoir and the blade edge runs in the liquid, which is picked up and transferred to the stone.

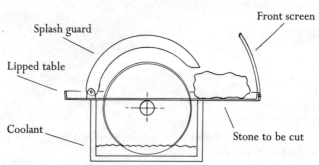

Coolant recommendations vary, but all lapidaries agree that water, although an excellent coolant, should be avoided, since it will cause rusting of the steel disc of the blade and probably the shaft as well. Paraffin and flushing oil, or a mixture of both, are frequently recommended, but they may be objected to on the grounds of smell as well as the difficulty of removing all traces of them from the stone.

My own preference is for soluble oil. This is used by machinists in engineering workshops and is diluted with about 10 parts of water. The oil readily mixes with water, forming a milky solution. It has the advantages of being very cheap, of washing away readily in water and of preventing any rusting.

Trimming saws consist, therefore, of a sump or reservoir to hold the coolant and a shaft with a pulley at one end to

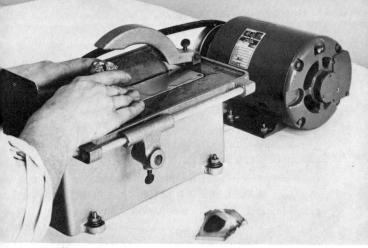

Above: Small trim saw. (*Gemrocks, London.*)

Below: 10-inch saw which can be used for both slabbing and trimming. (*Star Diamond Industries Inc., California, U.S.A.*; importers *Wessex Implex Ltd., Winchester, Hants.*)

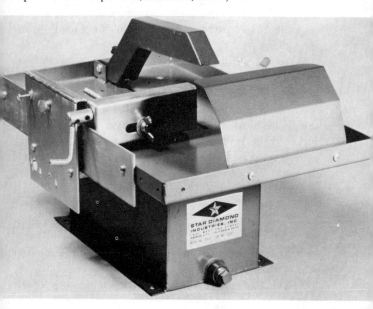

connect to a motor via a belt and a diamond blade at the other end. The blade projects through a slot in a table, which should have a lip around the edge and perforations over the sump to allow the coolant to return, and an adjustable splash guard over the blade.

Trimming saws, using a 6-inch or 7-inch diameter blade, are fairly easy for the enthusiastic amateur to build. The coolant reservoir must be waterproof, and the easiest way to ensure this is to make it of timber, $\frac{1}{2}$-inch plywood for example, and then to line it with fibreglass and resin. The table should be hinged to allow easy access to the blade and again can be made of plywood, covered either with sheet metal or with 'Formica'. The slot through which the blade projects should be about $\frac{3}{16}$ inch wide with $\frac{1}{4}$-inch diameter holes alongside for drainage.

The blade should be attached to a shaft running in two races of ball bearings. Manufacturers and suppliers of all equipment and parts mentioned will be found in the appendices.

Do not make the false economy of using a shaft with plain bearings. These rapidly show signs of wear, which induces rapid blade wear.

The table must be absolutely parallel to the longitudinal axis of the shaft in order that the blade will run at right angles to the table. Make sure, too, that the table is big enough to allow about 5 inches in front and on each side of the blade. Space to the rear of the blade, for obvious reasons, is not so important.

The speed of a diamond saw will vary according to the diameter of the blade. The optimum speed is 3000 surface feet per minute (s.f.p.m.). Revolutions can easily be found for any size of blade by dividing 3000 by the circumference of the blade in feet.

A 6-inch diameter blade has a circumference of πD

inches $= \dfrac{22}{7} \times 6 = 19$ in. Turning speed $= \dfrac{3000}{19} \times 12$

$= 1895$ r.p.m. A speed of 1800 to 2000 r.p.m. would be satisfactory, and this can be achieved by a simple arrangement of motor speed and pulley size (see Chart 1, page 127).

Trimming saws are used 'off-hand', that is the stone being cut is held and fed in by hand. This sounds rather terrifying, but there is nothing to worry about. Everyone knows that a woodworker's circular saw will whip off a careless finger in a flash, but a diamond saw is quite harmless and your finger can be held on the fast-spinning blade with absolute impunity. A demonstration will impress your friends no end.

Since a 6-inch trimming saw will project only about 2 inches above the table, this is obviously the limit of the depth of cut. In practice, one rarely uses a trimming saw for cuts thicker than 1 inch. Its chief diet is slabs from a slabbing saw and smaller pieces of stone about pebble size. Let us suppose that you have a slab (usually about $\frac{1}{4}$ inch thick) and that you want to cut an oval cabochon from it.

The slab will be carefully inspected on both sides to ensure that the best pattern is being used and also to prevent the inclusion of flaws. The shape required is marked on the slab using a template and scribing the line with a bronze or aluminium 'pencil' (the template and metal points will be dealt with more fully in the section on grinding – page 37). The slab will now look something like this:

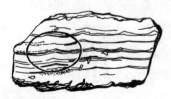

The lines for cutting are now scribed on the slab, leaving about $\frac{1}{16}$ inch clearance with the oval.

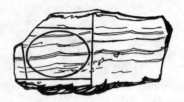

Switch on the saw, adjust the splash guard over the blade and ensure that a steady stream of coolant is travelling on the blade. Place the stone slab in front of the blade and align the first cutting line – the long one – with the blade, ensuring that the thickness of the blade is on the waste side of the line. Then, using gentle pressure with both hands, push the stone into the blade.

With gentle pressure maintained, the stone will pass steadily across the blade and the final $\frac{1}{8}$ inch will probably break away. Put the unwanted piece of the slab aside and then repeat the operation until you are left with a rect-angle containing the oval shape.

There are two ways to proceed. Either you can saw off the four corners to produce this effect or you can employ a 'nibbling' technique

and the resulting 'prongs' can be broken off with a pair of pliers. In either case the stone is now ready for grinding.

If you are intent on cutting your own slabs, then a slabbing saw will be needed. Slabbing saws, as previously mentioned, use blades of 10 inches diameter or bigger and they will require a mechanism for holding the rock firmly and sliding accurately across the blade. Such a mechanism is generally beyond the capabilities of most amateurs, but several quite effective designs have been made up by inventive amateurs with good workshop facilities.

The simplest form uses the weight of the stone to create the cutting pressure. The basic shape is similar to the trimming saw but scaled up to take a 10-inch or 12-inch diameter blade.

Along the front of the unit is mounted a length of heavy steel rod of round section. Sliding along this is an arm with a rock clamp at one end and a short length of tube at the other. The tube must be a good sliding fit on the rod. Also on the rod are two more pieces of heavier tube with locking screws to hold the arm steady, allowing it free swinging motion on a vertical plane but preventing it from moving along the rod.

A rock is mounted securely in the clamp and the arm positioned so that a slice can be removed as it gradually lowers itself onto the blade. When the rock is nearly sliced through, it is wise to feed the last $\frac{1}{2}$ inch or so by hand.

Plastic cover (could be metal
with plastic window)

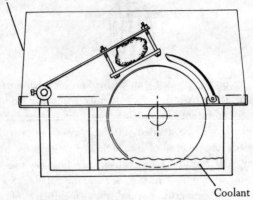

Coolant

Locking rings for positioning
swinging-arm rock clamp

First slice

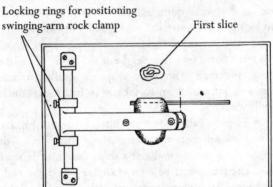

Simple, swinging-arm, gravity-feed slab saw.

When the first slice has been removed, the locking rings
are repositioned to allow another slice to be removed,
exactly parallel to the first. If the rock is properly positioned
in the clamp, it is possible to take five or six slices before
repositioning the rock.

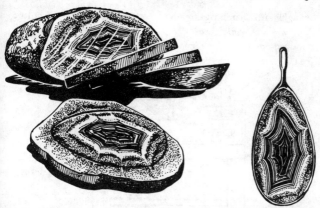

The second type of amateur slabbing saw uses a horizontal blade running inside a large pan.

Also inside the pan is a firmly fixed vertical shaft on which is lowered a sliding arm exactly like the clamp arm shown on the previous slabbing saw. Thick washers or short lengths of tube are placed on the shaft to bring the clamp to the correct height to take the first slice.

The clamp can be taken across the blade by hand pressure or by fixing a cord onto the clamp end of the arm, passing it over a pulley and attaching a weight on the end. Should you use this method, always be sure to use hand pressure on the last $\frac{1}{2}$ inch of cut, since the last $\frac{1}{8}$ inch or so of the cut will always break off, leaving a small projection to the main piece. If this is allowed to be pulled across the saw, it might well cause a slight buckling of the blade.

You will note that coolant cannot possibly be picked up by the blade in this method, and so it is necessary to fix up a coolant reservoir above the blade and to allow a small constant flow through a fine–bore tube and tap. A drain tube is fitted in the pan and the coolant is collected below for re-use.

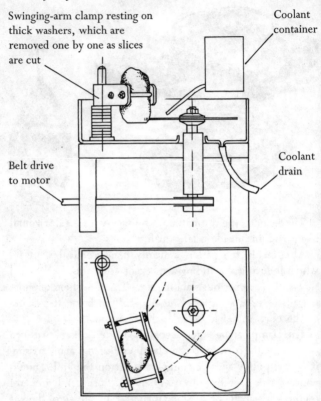

Swinging-arm clamp resting on thick washers, which are removed one by one as slices are cut

Coolant container

Belt drive to motor

Coolant drain

When the first cut has been made, the arm is lifted off the vertical rod and sufficient washers removed to give the required thickness of slab; the arm is then replaced and another cut can be taken.

It will be realised that, to ensure that the rock passes accurately across the blade, the vertical shaft must be absolutely at right angles to the surface of the saw blade. It must, in fact, be dead parallel to the shaft driving the blade.

Most pieces of gem material that will be slabbed are of irregular or rounded form and great care must be taken when introducing a stone to the saw to ensure that the blade is not forced out of line. You will see that, as the stone in the sketch is pushed into the blade, there will be a

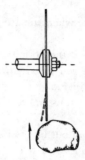

Heavy pressure at the start of a cut on a curving stone will tend to 'dish' the blade.

considerable tendency for the blade to slip to the left. If this is allowed to happen, it will cause 'dishing' of the blade.

To prevent this it is necessary to allow the blade to contact the stone lightly until it has cut a step, after which the blade will cut true.

Use gentle hand pressure until the diamond saw has cut a substantial 'step'.

Regardless of the method you employ to take a stone across a diamond saw, always start and finish with gentle hand pressure.

From time to time you will notice that a diamond saw blade that has plenty of cutting edge left is beginning to slow down on the job. Slabs take longer and longer to cut. This is particularly true when you are cutting a lot of agate or jade.

The blade segments in the periphery of the saw consist of powdered diamond and metal sintered together. After some use, the exposed diamonds become blunted and it will be necessary to expose some more. This process is called 'dressing the blade'.

The process is carried out by passing some soft, abrasive material across the blade. A soft building brick is suitable for this purpose and several cuts should be made through the brick to bring the saw back to cutting condition.

A worn-out lapidary grinding wheel is also good for dressing a diamond saw in the same way. But make sure that it is a lapidary grinding wheel (as will be specified in the next chapter) and not an engineer's grinding wheel.

Since lapidary is an ancient craft, newcomers are often at a loss to puzzle out the methods used in bygone days. The Chinese imported huge boulders of jade from Burma, and these were cut down into smaller and smaller blocks so that the exquisite jade carvings could be made. Jade has a hardness of $7\frac{1}{2}$ on the Mohs scale and, besides being very hard, is one of the toughest minerals known. How did they do it?

They used a method that is still used today for cutting up large rocks – the wire saw.

If several strands of soft-iron wire of about 0·030 inch diameter are twisted together and stretched on a frame like an ancient bow saw, you have the machine. A slurry of silicon carbide grit and water is placed on the rock and the wire is drawn backwards and forwards. The slurry is continually added so that the small recesses in the twisted wire pick it up and deposit it in the slowly deepening cut. From time to time fresh wires are stretched across the frame, preferably before the old wires wear down, break and jam in the same cut.

Eventually, with a great deal of effort, the rock is cut completely through. The old lapidaries had no silicon carbide and they employed crushed garnet as their abrasive medium, which must have tripled the labour.

The same principle of adding an abrasive slurry was used in early circular saws, when an iron or steel disc was rotated in a reservoir of water and silicon carbide which acted both as cutting medium and as coolant. These early saws were very slow and unbelievably filthy to use, thoroughly warranting their name of 'mud saws'. Present-day lapidaries can take great satisfaction in the advanced tools at their disposal.

Hints on diamond saws

Check that the saw rotates 'true' on its shaft. Any wobble can cause rapid wear.

Use steel flanges on either side of the blade. The diameter of the flanges must be at least a quarter, and preferably a third, of the diameter of the saw.

Always use a ball-bearing shaft to drive diamond saws and never use a shaft running in bronze bushes. The latter wear rather rapidly, allowing the blade to wobble.

Don't be in a hurry to push a stone across the diamond saw. Heavy pressure means rapid wear.

Always feed the start and finish of a cut by hand on a slabbing saw.

Start a cut very carefully on any diamond saw to prevent the saw slipping on the stone and causing dishing.

Never let a diamond saw run 'dry'.

If you build a saw yourself, avoid flimsiness of construction; always err on the robust side.

Shaft diameters: minimum size

Up to 6-in dia. blade $\frac{1}{2}$-in dia. shaft
Up to 10-in blade $\frac{5}{8}$-in dia. shaft
Up to 14-in blade $\frac{3}{4}$-in dia. shaft

Motor size

Up to 6-in dia. blade $\frac{1}{8}$ hp
Up to 10-in dia. blade $\frac{1}{4}$ hp
Up to 14-in dia. blade $\frac{1}{3}$ hp

If a hand-fed cut seems to be going away from the line, never try to twist the stone. Turn the stone around and start again from the other side.

Coolant is cheap, so clean out the sump frequently and replenish with fresh coolant.

4 Grinding Machines

All lapidary processes, with the exception of tumbling, involve the use of grinding wheels, and a good double-ended grinder is the most frequently employed machine in a lapidary's workshop. The basic grinder is similar to the machine found in any engineering workshop, but it has two major differences:

(1) The grinding wheels are made with a special 'soft bond'.

(2) The wheels must run wet.

Grinding wheels are made by mixing silicon carbide grits of a particular size with clay, which is moulded to shape and then baked. If the wheel is to cut soft material like steel, then the grits will hold their sharp edges for a long time and thus the wheel can be made with a hard 'bond' and will last a long time.

Conversely, if the wheel is to cut hard materials like gem stone, the grits will wear faster and therefore the wheel must be a soft–bond type so that fresh grits are constantly being exposed. This results in a faster reduction of the wheel, but you will still get good value from your wheel.

Soft-bond silicon carbide grinding wheels are invariably of a dull green colour, which makes them easily recognisable since hard-bond wheels are a dark grey colour.

The lapidary uses two grit sizes in his wheels. The coarse wheel is 100 grit and the fine wheel 220 grit. The commonest sizes are 8 inches diameter and 6 inches diameter. The thickness of the wheel should be as wide as possible, but the

Above: Small double-ended grinder. (*Gemrocks*, London.)

Below: Double-ended grinder with extended shaft for sanding and polishing. (*Gemstones*, Hull.)

chances of obtaining wheels wider than 1 inch are slim.

Grinding wheels are generally mounted in a vertical plane, except in some combination machines where the wheels can be mounted individually on a vertical shaft when the wheel operates in a horizontal plane. The vertically running wheels are much to be preferred, since the edge of the wheel is used.

A lapidary's grinding wheels must run wet, for two reasons. First, cutting on a grinding wheel creates considerable friction heat and this must be eliminated, since many gem materials are heat sensitive and could crack or even shatter if cut on a dry wheel. Secondly, the wet wheel prevents any stone dust from floating in the atmosphere. Breathing stone dust is unpleasant and some stones produce a dust that is positively harmful.

Lapidary grinding wheels, therefore, rotate inside capacious hoods which contain the water spray thrown off the wheel.

Home-made grinders are easily constructed, provided that one builds solidly and accurately around a heavy, ball-bearing, double-ended shaft with a central pulley.

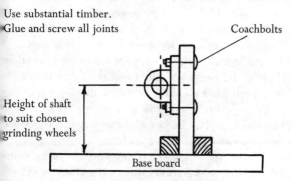

Use substantial timber.
Glue and screw all joints

Coachbolts

Height of shaft
to suit chosen
grinding wheels

Base board

The basic structure can be built of timber, provided that sturdy sections are used and care is taken to ensure that the various components are glued *and* screwed together solidly.

The shaft will look like this

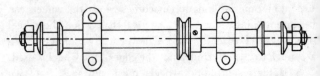

and must be fixed with bolts to the mounting board, taking care to put the driving belt on the pulley first.

There is always a little water spray around a grinder, so ensure that any wooden parts are conscientiously painted.

The hoods can be made of sheet metal carefully soldered at the seams or – and this method is surprisingly easy – they can be made of $\frac{1}{8}$-inch thick hardboard (masonite), which is then lined inside with fibreglass and resin and the outside coated with resin. Hoods made this way are incredibly strong, cheap and easy to make. The hardboard is cut accurately to size, and the pieces are held together with impact adhesive (Evostik or something similar) and with adhesive tape.

The structures are rather floppy in this condition, but when lined with fibreglass they become rigid and strong – certainly as strong as thin sheet steel or aluminium. I frequently stand on mine to demonstrate their strength.

The form and size of the hoods are not critical, but they should allow the hands virtually to work within them.

This is a left-hand hood for an 8-inch diameter grinding wheel; the right-hand hood will be a mirror image.

When the fibreglass has set (over night) the edges are trimmed and various refinements added.

These hoods are considerably bigger than many commercial grinders, which makes them more effective in use; commercial sizes are probably influenced by considerations of cost and compactness.

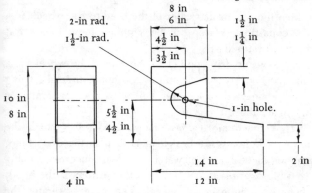

2-in rad.
1½-in rad.

10 in
8 in

4 in

8 in
6 in
4½ in
3½ in

1½ in
1¼ in

5½ in
4½ in

1-in hole.

14 in
12 in

2 in

Grinding hood.
This is the left-hand hood. The right-hand hood is a mirror image.
Where two dimensions are given, the larger will suit 8-inch
diameter grinding wheels and the smaller is for 6-inch diameter
grinding wheels.

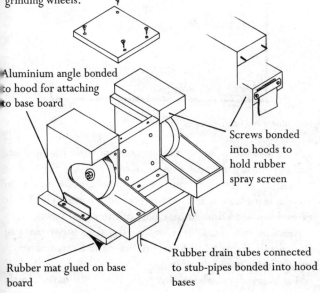

Aluminium angle bonded
to hood for attaching
to base board

Screws bonded
into hoods to
hold rubber
spray screen

Rubber mat glued on base
board

Rubber drain tubes connected
to stub-pipes bonded into hood
bases

Mention was made earlier of the need to run wheels in a wet condition. Water can be supplied in various ways, the two best being:

(1) A water drip applied to the top of the wheel via a tube passing through the top of the hood, the tube being either connected to a water tap or to a water container supported above the grinder.

(2) A much more convenient method, for which the home-made hoods are designed, is to plug the drain hole, pour in about $\frac{1}{2}$ inch of water and then squeeze a suitably sized block of plastic sponge into the bottom of the hood, underneath the grinding wheel. The water saturates the

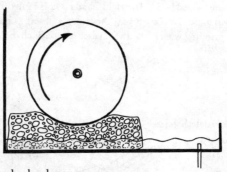

Grinding wheel and sponge.

sponge and the wheel rotates in contact with the sponge, picking up a continual film of water.

Whichever method you employ, be certain never to leave a stationary wheel in contact with water. The effect of so doing would be to have part of the wheel saturated in water and thus much heavier, locally, than other parts of the wheel. To switch a wheel on under these circumstances would be to court disaster.

Each grinding wheel that you buy will have clearly

marked on it its safe maximum speed of rotation, and this speed must never be exceeded. Fast running produces the most efficient cutting and one is tempted to run at high speeds, but good cutting is achieved by running 8-inch wheels at 2000 r.p.m. and 6-inch wheels at 2600 r.p.m., these speeds being well within the safe limit.

One more feature that should appear on a commercial grinder and therefore be incorporated in an amateur grinder is a platform for supporting flat stones when grinding to a profile.

This 'steady' or 'rest' should be mounted about $\frac{1}{8}$ inch below the horizontal axis of the grinding wheel and be

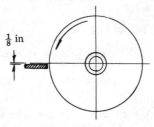

$\frac{1}{8}$ in

Position of 'rest' or 'steady' when grinding down to the line after trim-sawing. Maintain slight clearance between rest and grinding wheel.

adjustable so that it can just clear the wheel. The adjustment is necessary because the wheel reduces in diameter due to wear.

When Chapter 3 ended we were left with a stone that was cut from a flat slab. An oval cabochon was envisaged, that is a stone whose section is a smooth curve and whose plan (or top view) is a regular shape, in this case an ellipse. Cabochons can be round, square, oval, rectangular or any other shape you wish, but the section should be gently curved.

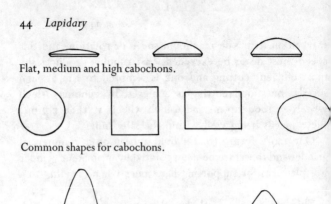

Flat, medium and high cabochons.

Common shapes for cabochons.

Common shapes for pendants.

Our stone in plan and section looks like this at present, so the first operation is to reduce the plan to a smooth oval or elliptic shape.

We start with the coarse (100-grit) wheel. Make sure that the wheel is running free and that adequate wetting is occurring. Place the stone flat on the rest and press gently into the wheel, moving it round gradually to create the desired form. Remove waste material evenly all round, bringing it gently down to the line.

When the grinding has reached the line, the stone can be transferred to the fine wheel, which will produce a smooth but unpolished surface around the oval. This is the limit of the grinding that can be done on a hand-held stone.

To produce the rounded section we have to mount the stone on a wooden rod so that we have perfect control over the stone as it is ground. The wooden rod is a 'dop stick', and the process of fixing the stone to the rod is called 'dopping' and uses 'dopping wax'.

Dopping wax is very similar to sealing wax but not quite so brittle. Any lapidary supply house will stock it, and it may be sold by the stick but more likely by the pound.

Dop sticks can be purchased, but since they are only lengths of dowel rod it is cheaper to buy 3-foot lengths of dowel rod of various diameters and cut them up into 6-inch pieces. The most usual diameters are $\frac{1}{4}$, $\frac{3}{8}$ and $\frac{1}{2}$ inch, but very small or large stones may require additional sizes.

Round one end of each piece on a sheet of glass paper; the other end can be left from the saw. The rounded end will be in the palm of the hand in use and the stone will be fitted onto the rough end.

The wax has to be melted and the stone heated simultaneously, so the same heat source can be used for both purposes.

The sketch shows the simplest way of heating the wax
and stones. A piece of sheet metal – steel or aluminium – is
bent as shown so that the top surface is about 4 inches square.
The height should be about 1 inch greater than the height
of a small spirit lamp.

A stick of dopping wax is broken up and the pieces put
in a small metal container – a tin lid is ideal – which is
placed immediately over the spirit lamp. The stones to be
dopped are placed alongside with a small crumb of wax
on each (when the crumb melts we know that the stones
are hot enough to be dopped).

Dop sticks should be selected so that the diameter of
the stick is about two-thirds the smallest dimension of the
stone. When the wax melts in its container, dip the end of
a dop stick into it, damp your fingers and mould the wax
on the end of the stick, spreading it along the last $\frac{1}{2}$ inch or
so of the stick.

When the crumb of wax on a stone melts, dip the end of

Prepared dop stick.   Stone applied. Check that the
                                       dop stick is perpendicular and
                                       central before putting aside to
                                       set.

a dressed dop stick vertically into the wax container, picking up a little additional wax. Press the stick vertically down on a stone, lift it up from the stove and press it down on a cold surface. Moisten your finger-tips and mould the wax so that it flows smoothly from stick to stone.

Check that the stone is well centralised and normal to the dop stick – that is, at right angles to the stick. You will have thirty seconds or so during which the stone can be moved gently in the setting wax. If it is necessary to re-position a stone after this, you will need to stand stone and dop stick upright on the dopping stove until the wax softens. When the stone is satisfactorily dopped, the stick should be placed in a rack to harden.

The rack can be a block of wood with holes drilled in it to hold the various sizes of dop sticks, or, more simply, a deep tray of sand. Ensure that the rack is large enough to hold a fair number of dop sticks, since it is useful to have stones in various stages of completion as well as spare dop sticks readily available.

Newly dopped stones should not be worked for several hours after dopping, which generally means leaving them overnight. The wax seems to toughen when left for some time.

We can now return to the grinder to continue the shaping of our original stone. The only modification necessary is to remove the rests in front of the wheels to give the required freedom of movement.

The dop stick is held in both hands, one supporting and one twisting the stick, in order to produce a small chamfer around the edge of the stone. This motion is repeated, holding the stone at a constant angle to the grinding wheel, until the stone reaches the shape shown in Figure A. Change the angle of the stone and take another chamfer cut to produce the shape in Figure B.

30° approx.

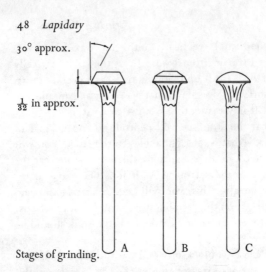

$\frac{1}{32}$ in approx.

Stages of grinding.   A   B   C

Now the motion becomes more complex as the stone is passed in curving sweeps across the wheel to convert the angles into smoothly flowing curves. Take particular care to remove the flat on the top and try to retain the $\frac{1}{32}$-inch base of the original shape. As long as this remains you can be sure that the stone keeps the shape originally selected, and it is also a help when the stone is being mounted.

The stone can now be taken to the smooth grinder and the shape refined. Any flats can be softened into curves and any ridges from the coarse grind can be removed. Inspect the stone frequently in a good light. Twist the dop stick so that the stone revolves slowly in front of your eyes. Check for symmetry across both ends.

Remember that future processes in polishing the stone can do very little to improve the shape. Whatever shape you have now is what you are going to finish up with. Never be in a hurry to get away from a fine grinder!

Although there is a great temptation to take one stone through all the processes in order to produce a beautiful finished gem, it is much more economical of time to take several stones through each process.

Care of grinding wheels

Grinding wheels should be used evenly over their full width, thus wearing them down evenly and economically and always presenting a flat surface to the gem stone. This is a counsel of perfection, of course, and the beginner will find, eventually, that the profile of the wheel looks like this:

Care of grinding wheels.

This may seem an ideal profile for grinding the curves of a cabochon, but it does produce problems. Eventually, portions of the sharp edges break away and the wheel, slightly out of balance, starts to 'bump'. This is a progressive fault which produces an increasing vibrating motion of the wheel and, indeed, of the whole machine. Long before this can develop into a dangerous condition the wheel must be dressed.

Dressing the wheel reduces it to a true circular form with a flat edge or profile. The easiest way to do this is to use a diamond dressing tool. This is not as expensive as it sounds, since it consists of a small industrial diamond soldered into

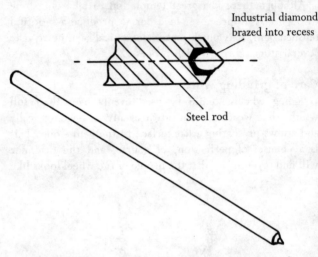

Industrial diamond
brazed into recess

Steel rod

Diamond dresser for truing-up silicon carbide grinding wheels.

a depression in the end of a steel rod. It will cost about £5, depending on the size of the diamond, and will last for ever.

To dress the wheel set up the rest, adjust the water, switch on the grinder and lay the dresser on the rest until it just starts to 'tick' against the high points on the wheel. Hold the dresser very firmly with both hands and slide it across the rest. A few minutes taking it back and forth across the wheel will bring the latter back into true circularity and flatness of profile.

When you have gained proficiency in using the grinder, you will find that you will need to use the dresser less and less.

A cheaper dresser consists of a steel bar into the end of which is set a number of serrated wheels of special tungsten steel. It is used in the same way as the diamond dressing tool. This type of dresser costs about £1, but the serrated wheels need to be replaced frequently and it ultimately costs more than the diamond dresser.

Eventually, after much grinding and some dressing, your grinding wheels will have reduced in size to a point where they are no longer convenient to use, and yet when you remove them for replacement you will see that only about one-third of the grinding wheel has been used. What to do? Assuming that you started off with 8-inch wheels, you will probably consider replacing them when they have reduced to about 6 inches diameter. A convenient solution is to have a second, smaller grinder which will accept the wheels too small to remain on the larger grinder.

Why a second grinder? Several reasons spring to mind. Very few men have ever set up a lapidary workshop without someone else wanting to get into the act. Wives and children are fascinated and eager to try their hands, and they are generally happier to start on smaller equipment.

Again, you will frequently find that you need a grinder for a few seconds, particularly when you are trim-sawing. It is often more convenient to set up a small grinder than a large one.

But the prime reason is the satisfaction of using grinding wheels economically. When they come off a small grinder, the wheels are reduced to about 3 inches diameter and are then ideal for dressing diamond saws. Even the pieces cut off when dressing the saws can be useful. They can be added to the first charge of a tumbler where they break down slowly, gradually adding new sharp grains of silicon carbide. Few things can have such a useful life as a thoroughly used grinding wheel.

Hints on grinders

Check a grinding wheel on purchase to ensure that it is not chipped on its periphery and that it is not cracked. Balance it on a finger-tip in the arbor hole and tap it with a metal rod or screwdriver. If it is sound it will 'ring', but if it is cracked it will 'clunk'. Reject any doubtful wheels and be careful not to drop a wheel that you have purchased.

Mount the wheels between flanges no smaller than a quarter the diameter of the wheels.

Make sure the wheels run true before using them for the first time.

Use heavy, ball-bearing shafts.

Don't overtighten the retaining nuts.

Keep rotation speed inside the safe limit.

Marking pencils for slabs are made of aluminium or bronze. They can be purchased or made from a length of welding rod. Use a bronze or aluminium welding rod about $\frac{1}{8}$ to $\frac{3}{16}$ inch diameter. Cut the rod into 6-inch lengths and file one end to a long, sharp point. Marking pencils will produce a gold or silver line which will not be washed away during the grinding process.

Templates of either metal or clear plastic can be purchased from lapidary supply houses. They are rectangular sheets with numerous cut-outs in various sizes and shapes (square, round, oval, rectangular, etc.).

5 Sanding and Polishing

One could make an analogy between working in gem material and working in wood. First the wood is sawn slightly over size, then it is planed to size and shape. Next it is sand-papered smooth and finally polished to a high lustre.

We have taken our gem stone through the equivalents of the first two processes and now we need to sand and polish it.

Sanding

Commercial machines are frequently made with an extended shaft having a trim saw at one end, two grinding wheels in the middle and a sanding/polishing wheel at the other end. There is much to be said for this type of machine. It is compact for such a multi-purpose machine and it is much cheaper than three separate machines.

It possesses several drawbacks, however. It is extremely heavy; it is difficult for two people to use simultaneously; and there is a serious risk of contaminating a polishing wheel, particularly, with grains of abrasive silicon carbide from a grinding wheel. Should this happen, a gem stone that has had a great deal of effort expended upon it is likely to finish up with so many deep scratches on it that it looks like an aerial photograph of Clapham Junction.

Separate machines obviate all these drawbacks, and for the person prepared to build his own machines the cost will be far less than the combination machine.

A sander/polisher is a very similar machine to the grinding machine, since it consists of a horizontal shaft driving two wheels which are running in hoods. The major difference is that the wheels are used on their sides, not their edges, and so the hoods are open-ended.

The base board and shaft mounting are identical to those shown for the grinder, but the hoods are simpler.

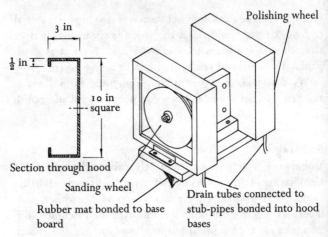

3 in

½ in

10 in square

Polishing wheel

Section through hood

Sanding wheel

Rubber mat bonded to base board

Drain tubes connected to stub-pipes bonded into hood bases

They consist of open-ended boxes, lipped all round the open side to prevent splash and capable of accepting 8-inch diameter wheels. They, too, can be made of sheet metal carefully soldered at the seams, or of hardboard and fibre-glass as described in the preceding chapter. Drain tubes should be set into the bottoms.

The complete machine is light and easily lifted into position. The hoods contain spray from the rotating wheels and also protect the polishing wheel, particularly, from contamination.

Sanding discs consist of discs of abrasive which look very similar to emery cloth. They must be waterproof, however, and are often known as 'wet and dry'. They are available in many grades of grit sizes, the most useful for our purpose being the 220, 400 and 600 grits. Again, these grits are silicon carbide, as used in tumbling and the manufacture of grinding wheels.

The cloth discs are quite expensive and you may be tempted to use paper discs, but you would be well advised to resist that temptation. Cloth discs outlive paper discs many, many times and are well worth the extra cost.

It is possible to make these cloth discs yourself, but home-made ones are seldom as good as the 'store-bought' items. To make them you will need some heavy cotton twill (the sort of material used to make blue jeans and overalls). Spread a sheet of polythene over a board and stretch the twill over this, pinning it down around the edge of the board. Brush on a good coat of a waterproof adhesive and, while it is still wet, sift on a coat of the required silicon carbide grit, using a flour sifter to ensure an even coat. Shake off any excess grit and leave to dry. Remove from the board, and on the reverse side mark off 8-inch diameter circles with a compass and cut out with sturdy scissors or snips.

To sand the smooth, curved tops of cabochons it is essential to have a resilient backing to the discs, and this is best achieved with a solid, wooden disc covered with plastic sponge sheet about $\frac{1}{2}$ inch thick.

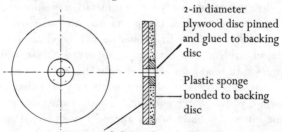

2-in diameter plywood disc pinned and glued to backing disc

Plastic sponge bonded to backing disc

Waterproof plywood or chipboard backing disc

Sanding wheel.

Cut out a disc of $\frac{1}{2}$-inch waterproof plywood or chip-board 8 inches in diameter with a centre hole to fit your shaft. Glue and pin a 2-inch disc, aligning its central hole with the hole in the 8-inch disc. This smaller disc should be the same thickness as the plastic sponge sheet. The plastic sponge disc should have a 2-inch hole cut in the centre and be glued to the larger wooden disc.

The small disc is to take the pressure of the flange and retaining nut, and to operate, the disc is slipped onto the arbor, followed by the sanding disc, which is held in place by the flange and nut. All the usable part of the sanding disc is now supported by a layer of sponge.

The sanding disc must run wet to prevent a rapid build-up of heat in the stone and to prevent any stone dust from floating around in the air. This poses quite a problem, since neither of the methods mentioned in the grinding section can be employed here. The water must be sprayed onto the face of the disc, and the usual method advocated is to have a squeeze bottle of water handy with which to apply the water. This entails a brief cessation of sanding, picking up the bottle, squeezing a jet of water on the disc, putting down the bottle and restarting the sanding. This has to be done every few seconds, and it is a miracle to me that anyone manages, this way, to sand a gem stone at all.

I recommend for your consideration a foot-operated water spray which is cheap and easy to make and works splendidly. It is built around a car windscreen-washer pump, which, in a car, has a dashboard button which is pressed to send a jet of water onto the windscreen.

Any car–accessory shop sells the kit, comprising the pump, plastic water container, plastic tubing and jet, and the parts are built into a simple foot-operated unit as shown.

The jet is clipped onto the hood of the sanding end of

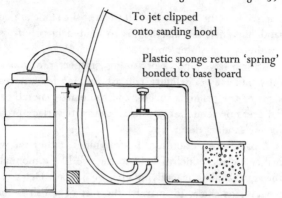

To jet clipped
onto sanding hood

Plastic sponge return 'spring'
bonded to base board

Foot-operated water jet based on car windscreen-washer kit.

the unit so that the stream of water hits the sander close to
the centre flange. Centrifugal force will spread it instantly
over the entire disc.

This method, as you will perceive, permits you to
concentrate your hands exclusively on the sanding of the
gems. An occasional pressure of the toe keeps the sanding
disc in prime condition.

Rotation speed of the sander should be about 2000
r.p.m., but the polishing disc at the other end must rotate
much slower. The motor driving the unit should have a
double or triple pulley so that quick and easy speed variations can be made.

The first sanding operation uses the 220 grit. The
appropriate disc is mounted, the motor started and several
jets of water directed upon the disc. The wet disc will
appear almost black. The dop stick is held in two hands
and the stone is drawn across the lower half of the wheel
against the direction of rotation. As it moves across the
disc, a turning motion is imparted to the dop stick and
successive strokes are made at slowly changing angles of the

dop stick to the disc so that all parts of the stone are equally sanded. When the disc begins to lighten in colour, squirt another jet of water on it.

After a few minutes of sanding, inspect the stone carefully under a good light. You are looking for any residual signs of the grinding wheel, and these are generally small, flat areas or scratches visible on the matt surface produced by the sanding disc.

A useful inspection tool is a magnifier, either the watchmaker's glass, which is held to the eye like a monocle, or the small folding magnifying glass or 'loupe'. Get a 10 or 8 power lens since, ultimately, the test of polish is that no scratches are detectable under such a lens.

Don't be in a hurry to change discs. Continue sanding until all traces of grinding are removed and the shape of the stone is symmetrical on both axes.

When you are ready to progress to a smoother disc, remove the nut and flange, take off the 220-grit disc and replace with the 400-grit. Go through the process again, this time removing all traces of the first sanding operation. Repeat this operation with the fine disc.

Often you will find that sanding discs are sold without a centre hole and it then becomes necessary to cut your own. Attempting to cut a hole of, say, $\frac{1}{2}$ inch diameter with a pair of scissors will rapidly convince you that there must be a better way. I suggest a simple punch. Find a piece of steel tube whose outside diameter is exactly the same as your shaft size. Cut off a short length, say 4 inches, and cut an internal chamfer on one end. This can be done with a small, half-round file, or with a small mounted grinding point which is sold in do-it-yourself shops. Choose the one shaped like a tiny Christmas tree. Mount it in an electric hand drill and it will cut the chamfer in seconds.

To use the punch place the sanding wheel over the sand-

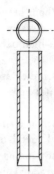

Hollow punch for cutting centre holes in sanding discs. Outside diameter must be the same as the sander shaft diameter.

Type of grinding point for cutting internal bevel in hollow chisel. Alternatively, use a small half-round file.

ing disc with the abrasive side down on a piece of waste wood. Place the punch in the arbor hole of the sanding wheel and strike it sharply with a hammer. This will cut a clean hole instantly in the centre of the disc.

You will find that unused sanding discs tend to curl

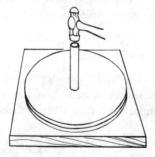

Place sanding disc on a piece of scrap wood. Cover precisely with sanding wheel. Use the centre hole in the wheel as a punching guide.

rather badly, so it is advisable to store them between two heavy pieces of wood, or between two discs of plywood or hardboard with centre holes through which pass a screw and winged nut.

Never discard used sanding discs until they are on the point of disintegrating. Some softer stones respond much better to a worn disc than to a new one.

Commercial sanding machines frequently use an adhesive to fix a sanding disc onto a sponge-faced metal disc. The adhesive is a non-setting type so that the sanding disc can be peeled off and replaced with the next grade. This method does have the advantage of having no centre nut, which eliminates the possibility of damaging a stone while sanding.

Another commercial sanding device is the drum sander. This appliance is a rubber-covered metal cylinder, either 2 or 3 inches wide, on which is slipped an abrasive band, and sanding is carried out in a very similar fashion to grinding. Sanding in this fashion has many devotees – especially in the United States where it originated – but in this country both the drum and the abrasive bands are rather expensive.

Whatever type of sanding you employ, always remember that another few minutes of sanding will almost certainly pay dividends.

Polishing

The other end of the sander/polisher is used exclusively for polishing and considerable care should be taken to ensure that no contamination with silicon carbide grits ever occurs.

Various materials can be employed as the surface of a polishing wheel, including felt, leather and several woven materials, but as a general-purpose surface leather is supreme.

Again it is necessary to provide a resilient surface to accommodate the curve of the cabochon, and a simple design is as follows. Start off with an 8-inch diameter disc of waterproof chipboard or plywood about $\frac{1}{2}$ inch thick with a central hole to suit your shaft. Cut an 8-inch circle of plastic sponge about 1 inch thick (or two circles $\frac{1}{2}$ inch thick) and cut a central hole about $2\frac{1}{2}$ inches diameter. Carefully bond the plastic disc onto the backing disc with impact adhesive, taking care to align the two centres.

Cut a 9-inch disc of soft leather with a 2-inch diameter hole in the centre. With the rough side outside, carefully tack the leather to the backing disc around the central hole. Then, stretching the leather carefully over the plastic sponge so that it takes up the form in the sketch, tack it down around the edge of the backing disc.

First stage
Bond plastic sponge to backing disc. Check concentricity of centre holes.

Second stage
Tack soft leather disc down around centre hole. Stretch uniformly over disc and tack down around edge.

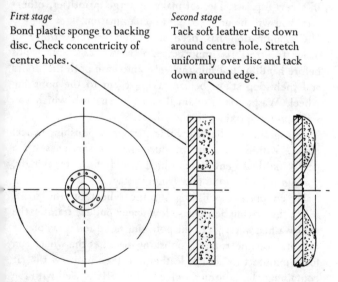

Polishing wheel.

Now, if you are a provident character, make a second one exactly the same.

The exposed centre of the polishing wheel should be big enough to accept a suitable flange and retaining nut.

The polishing media are the same as those specified in the section on tumbling (page 16). Cerium oxide and tin oxide are universal favourites, and you will find that some stones respond well to cerium and others to tin oxide – hence the suggestion that you should have two wheels. Be careful never to use both oxides on the same wheel, and store your polishing wheels in plastic bags when not in use.

The wheels will be easily recognised since tin oxide is a white powder and cerium oxide is orange coloured.

Make up a thin slurry of each oxide, using a teaspoonful of oxide and about an ounce of water, and keep these mixtures in screw-top jars. Do not make up large quantities, otherwise you will incur the risk of contamination.

Contamination has been mentioned several times in order to stress its importance. Always wash your hands before handling polishing wheels, and wash both the stones and their dop sticks before taking them to the polishing wheel. Wash, too, the small paint-brush with which you will apply the oxides to the wheel.

One grain of silicon carbide grit on a polishing wheel could, within seconds, produce several scratches on a nearly finished gem stone which could, heart-breakingly, consign it back to the fine-grinding stage.

To commence polishing set the wheel on the shaft, adjust the driving belt onto a low-speed pulley, transfer the well-washed water jet to the polishing hood and spray plenty of water on the rotating polishing disc. Let the wheel run for a minute to soak the leather and then unscrew the jar containing the polishing oxide slurry. Stir it well with the brush and paint a coat over the rotating wheel.

Take the dop stick in both hands – but this time make sure that the thumb and forefinger of one hand are high up, immediately beneath the stone. The motion of the stone on the polishing disc is similar to the twisting, curving strokes used on the sanding disc, but it is essential to use considerable pressure on the polishing wheel. Maximum polishing effect occurs as the wheel starts to dry; indeed, the pulling effect as the polishing occurs can readily be felt. Provided that the stone has been well prepared in the grinding and sanding processes, polishing will be completed in about half a minute.

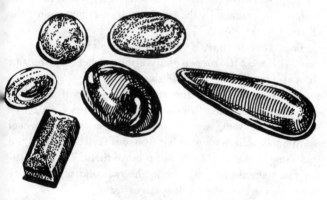

Polishing is quite magical and is not thoroughly understood. How, one asks, can a hard material like agate, capable of cutting glass with ease, be polished so readily using a soft leather and a wet slurry of a material (tin oxide) that looks and feels like flour?

The Beilby Flow Theory suggests that, because the metallic oxides used for polishing have higher melting temperatures than the stone being polished, there are set up in the tiny areas of contact enormous friction temperatures, which actually cause surface melting of the stone.

The molten stone is drawn over the surface, thus producing the glossy surface.

This theory may sound ridiculous to you, and I confess it did to me when I first heard it. However, in all fairness to Sir George Beilby, I have not heard of a more convincing one and until I do I shall remain a grudging Beilbyite.

Certainly a great deal of heat is produced, and you will find, if you are coaxing a polish on a reluctant stone, that the heat will penetrate the stone and soften the dopping wax. Always put this stone aside for a few minutes, or you may suffer the mortification of having to retrieve, from a corner of your workshop, a nearly finished stone which has been chipped or cracked by the impact as it was flung against the floor.

From time to time, if you are polishing a batch of stones, you will need to dampen the polishing wheel and repaint it with freshly stirred oxide slurry.

Polishing does have the regrettable habit of revealing hitherto unsuspected flaws and defects. It may be a bitter blow to see some scratches left from a grinding wheel spoiling an otherwise glowing, lustrous surface, but all the polishing in the world will not remove them. That particular stone should be put back in the rack and subsequently taken through *all* the sanding stages again.

It has been assumed throughout this lengthy dissertation that the stone being cut and polished is an opaque stone – an agate or jasper, perhaps – and consequently the base of the stone will not need to be polished. It can be left from the saw or given the minor treatment outlined later. Eventually, of course, you will be working with transparent gems such as amethyst or citrine and then the base will need to receive the same careful treatment as the top. Grinding and polishing flat surfaces present peculiar problems of their own and will be dealt with in the next section. This section will conclude with a description of the treatment of the opaque cabochon.

The first problem is to separate the stone from the dop stick to which it has been attached for so long. Place it in the freezer compartment of your refrigerator for five minutes and it will pop off easily with gentle pressure – that is, if it hasn't actually fallen off in the refrigerator. The alternative method, if the kitchen is too far away, is to warm the wax over the flame of the dopping lamp – or a match. The stone will then pull off easily and the residual wax can be either scraped off with a knife or rubbed off against a piece of glass paper laid on the bench.

The base of the stone is – or should be – quite flat from the saw but unpolished. The surface can be improved by holding the stone, in the fingers, flat against the side of the smooth grinding wheel as it rotates. Use the foot spray to wet the side of the wheel and slide the stone off the wheel, rather than try to pick it off with finger pressure.

Another refinement is to grind a tiny bevel around the base of the stone, employing part of the $\frac{1}{32}$ inch of stone that was left unground in the initial shaping. This will

Chamfer on stones.

greatly facilitate the mounting of the stone in the bezel of a ring or other piece of jewellery. This, too, can easily be achieved with hand-held grinding.

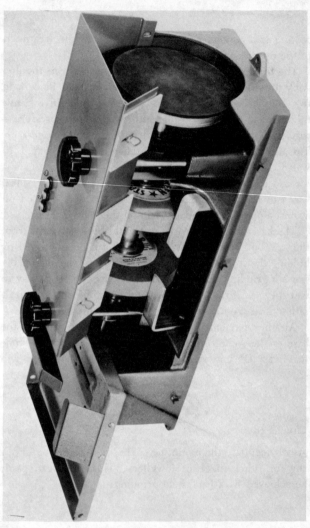

Combination machine using 6-inch diameter wheels and saw.
(*Star Diamond Industries Inc.*, *California*, *U.S.A.*; importers *Wessex Implex Ltd.*, *Winchester*, *Hants.*)

6 Combination Machines

The various operations described in the preceding chapters – sawing, grinding, sanding and polishing – are the most frequently used by the amateur lapidary. Consequently, the makers of machines for lapidaries concentrate much of their output in these areas. The growing tendency is to produce a machine on which all these operations can be performed, and if you propose to equip a lapidary workshop in a limited area you will certainly need to consider the various combination machines.

They fall into two main types: the horizontal-shaft machine and the vertical-shaft machine.

The horizontal-shaft machine operates, along its length, a trim saw, one or two grinding wheels, one or two sanding drums and a polishing disc.

Trim saw   Grinding wheels   Sanding wheels   Polishing disc

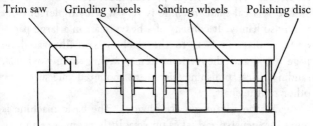

Typical combination machine layout.

The advantages of such a set-up are immediately apparent. There is no changing from one machine to another. You can proceed from rough slab to finished cabochon by progressing steadily from left to right. It is almost certainly cheaper to buy a single machine such as this than to purchase three or four separate machines. The whole thing will be less than 4 feet long and is operated by a single motor.

The disadvantages are less obvious. Changing a grinding wheel or a sanding drum can be a tedious job on a combination machine, involving in some cases a considerable amount of dismantling.

Bearings on such a machine tend to need replacing much more frequently than do the bearings on single machines. This is partly due to the design problems inherent in such a machine but mostly due to the fact that *all* the bearings are being used *all* the time, whereas with single machines only the machine you are actually using is being subjected to wear.

It is not always convenient, despite its length, for two people to work on the combination machine at the same time. With separate machines this problem does not exist.

The possibility of contaminating the polishing section with stray grains of silicon carbide from the grinding and sanding sections is an ever-present hazard.

The vertical-shaft machine is very much simpler but not nearly so handy. It consists of a heavy shaft in a large pan – quite similar, in fact, to the slabbing saw illustrated on page 32 – and the various items, saw, grinding wheels, sanding discs, polishing discs, are mounted one after the other on the shaft.

Again, the advantages are obvious. The basic machine is quite inexpensive and takes up very little room. Even more operations can be carried out on it than on the horizontal-shaft combination machine, since it is possible to use it as a slabbing saw, a grinder, a sander, a polisher, a lap and even as a facetting machine.

Some disadvantages are also obvious.

It takes quite a while to change it from one function to

another, especially when fitting a diamond saw or a grinding wheel since these should always be checked to ensure that they are running dead true.

Storage space for all the spare wheels etc. tends to cut into the initial space-saving of the basic machine.

Contamination in the polishing stage is likely even with scrupulous care being taken.

Grinding on a horizontal wheel presents problems which just don't occur when grinding on a vertical wheel.

If you are beginning to suspect that I am less than wildly enthusiastic about combination machines, then I may as well confess that this is so. It is undeniably true that they have several considerable advantages, but it is equally true that a machine that sets out to perform several different functions rarely performs any of them as well as specialist machines of the same calibre.

Should limitations of space be your first consideration, however, you may well find that a combination machine will serve you well.

Above: Vibrating lap. (*Star Diamond Industries Inc.*, *California*, *U.S.A.*; importers *Wessex Implex Ltd.*, *Winchester*, *Hants.*)

Below: Rotating lapping machine with built-in motor. (*Gemstones*, *Hull.*)

7 Lapping

Many lapidaries become so entranced with the patterns revealed when a rock is slabbed that they wish to grind and polish the flat surfaces and to make a display feature of a collection of such slabs. Such an operation is difficult, if not completely impossible, on the equipment previously described, and so a further piece of equipment becomes necessary.

A flat grinding machine is called a lap and, to add to the confusion, this word also springs from the same root as the word 'lapidary'. Both of them originated from the Latin word for stone – *lapis*.

The most spectacular machine available commercially is the vibrating lap. In this machine a flat plate of metal, heavily grooved and generally made of an aluminium/copper alloy, vibrates in a horizontal plane inside a cushioned fence. A mixture of quite coarse silicon carbide grit and water is spread on the metal plate and then the flat stones are placed face down on the plate. When the motor is switched on, the plate vibrates in a rapid but low-amplitude oscillation. The stones, due to inertia, tend to stay where they are and the plate vibrates underneath them, carrying the grit backwards and forwards in a highly efficient grinding action.

The stones do, in fact, shuffle aimlessly about the plate very slowly, but the cushioned fence keeps them on the lap; as the hours pass in this unsupervised operation, the grits break down finer and finer, so that there is an automatic progression of grit sizes from coarse to fine.

Eventually, the stones are ready for polishing. The plate

and the fence are washed clean, as are the stones, and then the plate is covered with a woven-material polishing cloth. This is painted with a slurry of cerium oxide or tin oxide and water, and the stones are replaced for an hour or so of polishing.

Very effective; but some lapidaries tend to miss the personal involvement – the 'alone I did it' syndrome – and for these dedicated workers a much simpler lap is available.

This consists of a deep tray inside which rotates – relatively slowly – a cast-iron disc from 6 to 12 inches in diameter.

Successively finer slurries of silicon carbide grits and water are brushed onto the plate, and the slabs or other flat surfaces are held by hand and moved in gentle, swinging arcs over the entire surface of the plate. Careful washing of the plate, the slab and the hands is essential between each grit change, and some particularly fastidious lapidaries even line the tray with newspaper, which is replaced with each grit change.

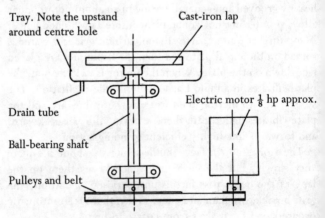

Tray. Note the upstand around centre hole

Cast-iron lap

Drain tube

Electric motor $\frac{1}{8}$ hp approx.

Ball-bearing shaft

Pulleys and belt

Schematic layout of a lapping machine.

When the stones have been taken down to 600-grit slurry they are ready for polishing. Either a thin, flat plate of metal covered with leather or fine felt is clipped onto the cast-iron plate, or the lap is removed and another plate, similarly covered, is screwed onto the shaft. As before, following careful washing, a cerium or tin oxide slurry is used as the polishing medium and the slabs are polished by hand pressure.

Readers will recognise that this is an ideal machine for grinding and polishing the flat bases of cabochons made from transparent gem stone. If the stone is too small to be hand-held without getting an impromptu manicure, then the stone should be reverse-dopped and the dop stick held

Polishing base of stone.

very close to the stone. Be sure to grind the tiny chamfer around the base edge first, however, or you may get a series of minute chippings breaking away from the edge. The chamfer can be cut and polished on the lap.

Laps of this type are very easy to make, since all that is required is a single-ended shaft with a threaded portion at one end and a pulley at the other. The lap plate should be of cast iron – although it is only fractionally better than a steel plate – and should have a centre boss drilled and threaded to fit onto the shaft. The plate should be at least $\frac{1}{2}$ inch thick.

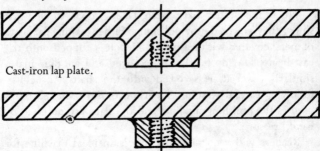

Cast-iron lap plate.

Fabricated mild-steel lap plate with suitable nut welded or brazed into position.

Because the outside of the lap travels faster than the centre, it cuts faster and wears faster. Eventually your lap will have a raised centre, and when this is noticeable the

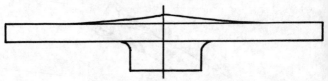

Exaggerated view showing uneven wear on a lap plate after much use. Long before this state is reached, the lap should be machined flat.

lap must be machined true and flat again. Hence the necessity of starting off with a good thickness to your lap.

Its rotation speed will depend on its diameter. 200 to 300 r.p.m. is suitable for an 8-inch lap and 150 to 200 r.p.m. for a 10-inch lap. This means that motor speed must be considerably reduced by pulley ratio. If, for instance, your motor runs at 1420 r.p.m. (a standard speed) and you have an 8-inch lap, you will need a $1\frac{3}{4}$-inch motor pulley driving a 9-inch shaft pulley to produce a lap speed of 275 r.p.m.

A lap is well worth its place in any lapidary shop. It has

many uses and applications which, coupled with a low initial cost and negligible running costs, make it extremely good value for money.

Recently a considerable amount of publicity has been given to a process of cutting the tops off bottles to make tumblers, vases, etc. Very little publicity was given to the drudgery of grinding and polishing the cut edges of these objects before they could be used. It appears that the makers of the glass-cutters employed suggested that sheets of 'wet and dry' paper should be spread on a flat surface and the cut edges rubbed and rubbed and rubbed until all roughness vanished. A small lap does this job in minutes. It can also put a chamfer around the edge and then polish the new surfaces too.

The bases of glass decanters, bowls, vases, etc., become very scratched in use and they benefit greatly from a few minutes on a lap. Anything, in fact, that is reasonably hard can have flat surfaces cut or restored on this versatile little machine.

Some gem materials have inclusions in a transparent material which look exquisite if cut into very thin, polished slices. Moss agate, rutilated quartz and tourmalinated quartz are good examples.

Other materials, notably jade, are almost opaque in the chunk but reveal delightful colours when in thin slices. Some otherwise ordinary agates reveal the most glorious light changes when a thin slice is inspected against a distant light source. These are known as iris agates.

The problem is not cutting the thin slices, since any decent slabbing saw should be capable of taking slices as thin as $\frac{1}{16}$ inch. The difficulty is experienced in grinding and polishing. The answer lies in fixing the slab to a firm backing, which will enable the slab to be easily manipulated and also prevent accidental damage.

A piece of wood about an inch thick is ideal, and it should be cut to the shape of the slab so that all parts are supported but with a minimum of inconvenient overhang. For grinding, beeswax is suitable as a bonding agent. Coat the surface of the wood with warmed, molten beeswax and warm the stone to about the same temperature. Place the stone in position on the wooden backing and then put the assembly, stone down, on a cool surface until the wax has set.

The slab can now be lapped through the various grit stages before warming the slab and reversing it in order to grind the reverse side.

Beeswax, unfortunately, is unlikely to hold when the slab is being polished because of the considerable heat produced in the polishing process. Any adhesive that is not heat sensitive is rather a nuisance when it comes to separating the stone from the backing.

My choice falls between ordinary dopping wax for small-area slabs and 'impact adhesive' – the sort used for fixing plastic laminate sheet on table tops etc. – for slabs bigger than about 2 square inches in area.

When using dopping wax, the wood and the stone must be warmed and coated with wax before placing them together. It is as well to place the assembly face down on the dopping stove to ensure good bonding before sliding it off onto a cool surface. With such a large contact area you can start polishing as soon as the stone is cold. Remove the stone with heat, reverse, and clean off the residual wax before polishing the second side.

When larger stones are bonded with impact adhesive, it is only possible to separate the stone from its backing by means of the appropriate solvent. (The adhesive manufacturers supply the correct solvent for removing excess adhesive from the job and hands.) It will be necessary to soak the block and the slab in the solvent until they separate, and this may take hours. With large slabs, leave them immersed overnight and resist sternly the temptation to pry the slab loose with a screwdriver or cold chisel.

8 Drilling

The drilling of gem stones is occasionally necessary – for example, when using them as beads, when inserting a ring to suspend a gem stone as a pendant and when inserting pegs for specialised mountings.

It is an art as old as lapidary itself, and the Chinese are adepts at drilling fine holes using a needle rotated in a small bow and employing crushed diamond dust as the cutting medium. This method requires years of practice to develop sufficient skill and is not recommended to the tyro lapidary. Other methods, however, are much more easily learnt.

Holes can easily, if not quickly, be cut using a length of fine-metal tube or rod rotated in a fast-turning electric drill and employing silicon carbide grits to provide the cut. Holes from $\frac{1}{16}$ to $\frac{1}{8}$ inch diameter can be achieved in this manner and are suitable for most purposes.

The drill should be either a small press drill or an electric hand drill mounted in a press–drill stand, which the drill manufacturers provide as an accessory. It should run at a high speed, preferably between 4000 and 5000 r.p.m. It should also be in good condition with no wobble in the chuck.

The metal tube or rod can be of stainless steel, steel, brass or bronze and should be about 2 inches long with the end squared off. If you use a rod, it is advisable to file it gently while it is rotating to produce the shape shown. This ensures that the rod does not jam as the hole deepens.

The easiest stone to drill, and therefore the one to be

Drill made from metal rod.

The undercut is filed in as the rod rotates in a drill. Maximum hole size for a rod drill is about $\frac{1}{8}$ inch. Over this size, a tube drill is faster.

described, is a flat, parallel-faced slab. The slab should be fixed with dopping wax or beeswax to a block of wood larger than itself so that the wood can be clamped to the bed of the drill.

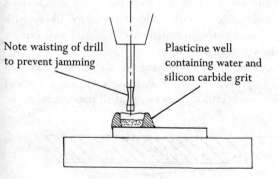

Note waisting of drill to prevent jamming

Plasticine well containing water and silicon carbide grit

Set-up for drilling with a metal rod.

The slab is bonded to a piece of smooth, parallel-faced wood with wax. The wood is clamped to the bed of the drill.

A fence has to be placed around the hole in order that the drill can run in a slurry of silicon carbide grit and either water or oil. The fence can either be moulded from modelling clay or a large nut can be fixed on with dopping wax. The latter, though slightly more time-consuming, is less liable to come adrift halfway through the proceedings.

The block/stone/fence assembly is clamped to the bed of the drill and a check made that the drill will enter at the precise point required. A pinch of silicon carbide 220 grit is placed inside the fence and a few drops of water or thin oil are added (oil, being thicker than water, is less likely to be flung out by the rotating drill).

Switch on the drill, check that the rod or tube is running true and bring it down very gently into the slurry-filled fence. Allow it to touch the stone with gentle pressure for a few seconds and then lift it a fraction of an inch. This process of gentle contact for a few seconds and a momentary lift is continued in order that the grains under the drill are frequently replaced. Do not expect rapid results. If you can cut through a $\frac{1}{4}$-inch slab in five minutes it must be a softish stone. Six or eight minutes is more likely with quartz, while the tougher materials like agate and, especially, jade will take even longer.

A secondary effect of dopping the slab onto a block of wood is to prevent rough breakthrough when the edges of the hole are crumbled away as the drill penetrates. Some

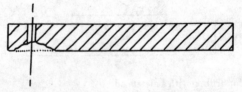

Typical break-out fracture when stone is unsupported or too much pressure is used.

slight roundness of the exit hole may exist and it is advisable, if you can sense when you have nearly penetrated, to reduce the pressure on the drill.

To finish off a hole a sort of countersinking is advisable. Make up a countersinking tool from $\frac{1}{4}$-inch diameter metal and file the end while it is rotating in the drill to a conical point.

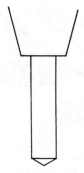

Countersinking bit for bevelling the edges of drilled holes. Brass, mild steel and dural are the best materials.

When the slab has been removed from the block, support it on a piece of wood, smear a grinding paste of 220-grit silicon carbide and grease on the conical tip of the tool, and bring the rotating tool gently down into the hole, pressing and lifting as before until a small chamfer is cut around the lip of the hole. Reverse the slab and repeat the process.

You will find that you will not be able to cut many holes with a drill before it needs replacing, but the cost and time of replacement is very small compared with the time employed in drilling a hole.

If you need to drill a large number of holes, then you will require a diamond drill. These are generally available in

two types. The cheaper of the two is a steel rod, the business
end of which is shown below.

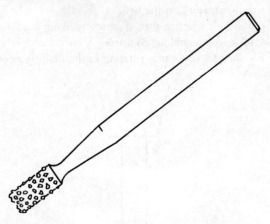

Diamond drill.
The steel core is rolled in crushed diamonds, which are held in
place by heavy plating.

The parallel portion is rolled in crushed diamond and the
fragments are held in place by an electrolytic deposition of
chromium. The second type is similar in appearance, but the
end is a small sintered cylinder of diamond and metal
identical in composition to the blocks on the rim of a
diamond saw. This cylinder is hard-soldered to the drill
shaft to form an efficient, long-lasting, but rather costly,
little tool.

Using a diamond drill makes the fence redundant. It
will still be necessary to use a coolant, but water can most
effectively be added with a small brush. The absence of the
fence makes it much easier to inspect the hole, and since
the duration of the drilling period is so much shorter
many lapidaries hold the stone in position by hand on a

block of wood and, when the hole is almost complete, turn the stone over and complete the hole from the other side. The nearly completed hole is clearly visible from the reverse side on even the most opaque materials. This technique obviates the very real risk of a rough break-through of the drill when going straight through.

Many shapes of small diamond tools are available (they are used primarily for gem-stone carving) and the small conical tool used for bevelling the edges of the hole can be readily obtained if required.

If a large hole (bigger than $\frac{3}{16}$ inch dia.) is required, a core drill will be necessary. Core drills can be of any diameter and basically of the same construction. The drill consists of a metal tube fitted to a rod which is gripped in

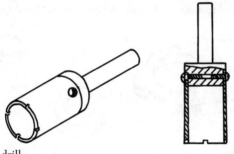

Core drill.
The notches on the rim maintain a supply of grit in the cut.

the drill chuck. Home-made core drills need a competent machinist and a good lathe. Solid–drawn, thin-wall steel tube is required, and the mandrel is made so that the tube is a good press fit on the shaft, as indicated. Commercial core drills will be diamond-impregnated around the end of the tube, and amateur drills can be pressed firmly in crushed diamond (available by the carat at surprisingly reasonable cost from lapidary supply houses) or else used inside a fence with 220 grit and water.

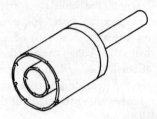

An interesting variation on the large core drill is the double or concentric core drill, which has two tubes, one inside the other. This is used when rings are being made from solid gem-stone material, particularly jade. One, rather long, cutting operation will produce a ring ready to be ground to shape and a circular stone ready for dopping.

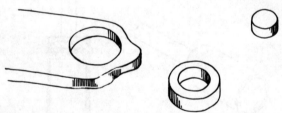

Double core drill.
This device is very useful for making gem-stone rings. A tough stone like jade is used. The round cabochon preform is a bonus.

Large drills run at slower speeds than small ones, so by the time you reach 1-inch diameter holes the drill should be running at less than 1000 r.p.m. A very useful attachment to use on an electric hand drill is a thyrister speed controller, which is a small electronic device that can vary the speed of the drill steadily from maximum down to very slow without seriously affecting the drill's power output. This device will only work on electric motors fitted with carbon brushes, and disaster will attend its application on any other type of electric motor. Fortunately, all electric hand drills use this type of motor.

9 Facetting

The most popular of the advanced lapidary techniques is facetting. In this work a transparent gem stone has regular flat facets cut and polished over its entire surface to reflect light and to add colour and brilliance to the finished gem.

Only flawless material is suitable for this treatment, which can involve considerable expense if it is proposed to use ruby, emerald or sapphire, but there is plenty of less costly stone that can be turned into exquisite gems.

The quartz family provides rock crystal (water clear), rose quartz (delicate pink), amethyst (mauve to deep purple), citrine (golden) and smoky quartz (golden brown), all of which are available in facetting grades at moderate prices.

The precision used to cut and polish the facets would make a toolmaker blench. The techniques used by professionals take years to learn, but amateur lapidaries have, over the last decade or so, developed machines and equipment so accurate that the only attributes necessary to make an acceptable facetted gem are the desire to succeed and a fair amount of patience.

Understandably, these machines are expensive, particularly so since they are all imported into Britain – from America chiefly, though some superb machines are now coming from Japan. At a rough estimate, it would cost about £300 to equip your workshop with a facetting machine and its accessories.

Space limitations prevent more than a brief survey of facetting techniques in this introduction to lapidary, and readers interested in this aspect of lapidary are advised to consult the Bibliography at the end of the book to discover sources of further information.

Before facetting can commence it is necessary to grind the gem material to the shape of the required gem. This is known as preforming.

Stages of preforming for a brilliant-cut stone. Step-cut preform.

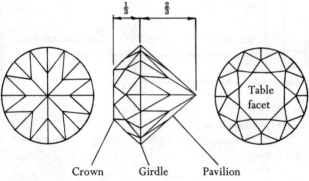

Crown   Girdle   Pavilion

Brilliant cut.

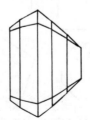 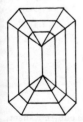 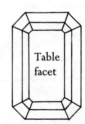

Step or emerald cut.

The process is best described by outlining the technique employed on a very simple apparatus known as the 'O'Brien Facetter'.

The machine consists of a master lap supporting a diamond-coated copper lap and an adjustable table.

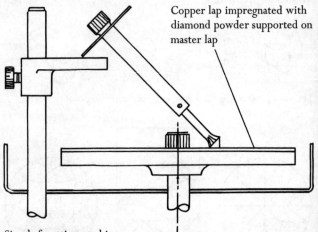

Copper lap impregnated with diamond powder supported on master lap

Simple facetting machine.
Adjustable table supporting template and giving correct angle for facet-cutting.

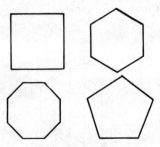

Templates can be any regular shape. They should be cut from sheet metal thick enough to ensure stiffness.

The preform is fixed with dopping wax to a metal dop stick, ensuring that it is accurately centred and aligned. To the other end of the dop stick is fixed an accurately shaped metal template, which can be square, rectangular, hexagonal, octagonal or any other regular geometric polygon. This, too, must be aligned with the axes of the preform.

The height of the table is adjusted to provide the correct angle of the first major facet and then, with the correct edge of the template resting on the horizontal table, the stone at the other end is moved gently over the rotating lap until, after constant inspection, the facet is sufficiently cut. Now the template is rotated until the opposite, identical, facet surface is in contact with the lap, and the facet is cut until it appears, under close inspection with a high-powered lens, to be identical to the first. This process is repeated until all the series of identical facets are cut. The height of the table is then adjusted until a secondary series of facets can be cut by the same technique.

When all the facets are cut on the bottom or 'pavilion' of the gem, the diamond cutting lap is replaced with a polishing lap and the position of the table is carefully adjusted to enable all the facets to sit flatly in sequence on the new lap.

Various polishing laps are suggested by different authorities, including tin and lead laps which consist of a disc of tin or lead which is bonded to a master lap, generally aluminium alloy. The lead or tin laps must be turned on a lathe after casting and are not easy to make.

A very successful lap for all but large gems is made of a disc of perspex, preferably about $\frac{1}{2}$ inch thick to prevent any curvature developing under polishing pressures. Two or more thinner sheets can be bonded together.

The perspex lap is mounted on the master lap and a thin

mixture of cerium oxide and water is painted on. The facets are polished individually until close inspection with a 10 power lens shows no scratches.

Careful experimentation will show which technique suits any particular gem. Some stones prefer one direction of rotation to the other. Some only polish successfully when the lap is on the point of drying out. In any case, swing the gem gently over the entire surface of the lap to prevent any local grooving.

When the polishing procedure is completed it is necessary to reverse the stone, and this has to be done extremely accurately in order to maintain the vertical axis through the stone and also to align the crown and pavilion facets.

A transfer jig is essential for this reversal.

(1) Place the dopped stone into one side of the transfer jig and lock it in position.

(2) Heat another dop stick designed to fit the pavilion of the gem and well coated with dopping wax. Slide it along the groove until it is hard against the pavilion end of the stone. Lock down this dop stick and mould the wax well around the gem. Leave to cool with both dop sticks firmly attached to the stone.

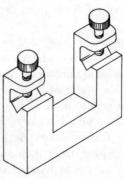

Transfer jig.

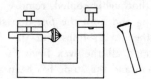

First stage

After cutting pavilion, mount dop stick in transfer jig and tighten
screw to lock in position. Heat and wax second dop stick.

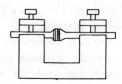

Second stage

Slide second dop stick into position against the gem stone and
lightly tighten screw.

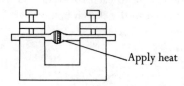

Apply heat

Third stage

Apply heat where indicated to make the wax plastic. Push hard
against the end of the dop stick, tighten screw and mould wax onto
gem stone. Leave to set.

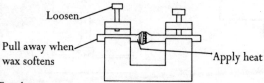

Loosen

Pull away when
wax softens

Apply heat

Fourth stage

Loosen screw. Apply heat where indicated until wax softens;
pull away original dop stick. Clean wax from exposed stone; set up
in facetter for cutting the table.

(3) When thoroughly cooled, remove the assembly from the transfer jig and hold the *first* dop stick over a spirit flame until the wax softens and the dop stick can be removed. Scrape all the wax from the exposed, uncut, end of the gem and the stone has been successfully transferred.

The template is fixed to the end of the new dop stick and the flats carefully aligned by sighting with the facets already cut on the pavilion. The crown facets can now be cut in sequence and then polished.

This leaves only one facet to be cut, the large top or 'table' facet. Obviously, the dop stick must be vertical in order to cut this facet, and with the equipment so far described this is not possible. A small block with holes to take two dop sticks is employed. The holes are drilled at a 45 degrees angle to each other and the two dop sticks are used as shown in the sketch below.

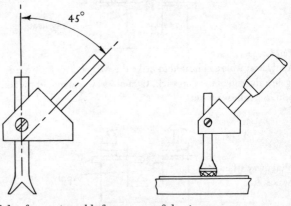

45° dop for cutting table facets.   45° dop in use.

The facetting arm protractor is set to 45°. The angled dop ensures the big table facet is cut accurately and without judder.

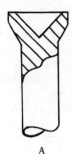  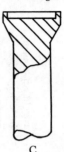

A   B   C

Basic dop shapes:
A 'Conical' for holding the pavilion of round 'brilliant-cut' stones.
B 'V-groove' for holding either side of 'step-cut' or 'emerald-cut'
   stones.
C 'Flat-top' for holding the crown of 'brilliant-cut' stones.
A dop should be selected for size as well as for shape.

As long as the height of the table is adjusted so that the
dop stick resting on it is at an angle of 45 degrees, then
the second dop stick will be perpendicular to the lap and
the table facet can be cut and polished.

The more complex – and more expensive – facetting
machines used by many amateur lapidaries enable facet
angles and rotation angles to be set with great accuracy.
Once, for instance, a crown main facet has been cut satisfactorily, all the other crown mains can be cut with certainty
and exactitude.

Amateur construction of facetting machines will depend
on your capabilities and facilities. The lap and table method
requires merely that the table is always absolutely parallel
to the revolving lap, but it is really only suitable for fairly
simple facetting since every facet has to be judged by eye.
It is, however, an excellent introduction to facetting and
is to be recommended before involving yourself in the

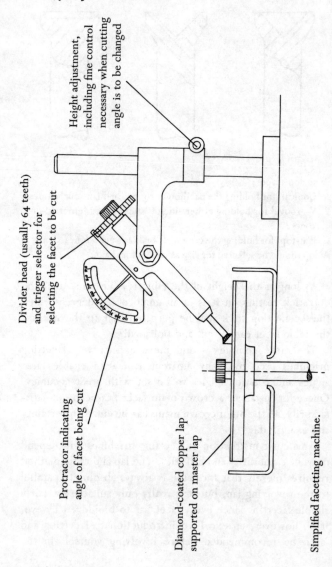

Height adjustment, including fine control necessary when cutting angle is to be changed

Divider head (usually 64 teeth) and trigger selector for selecting the facet to be cut

Protractor indicating angle of facet being cut

Diamond-coated copper lap supported on master lap

Simplified facetting machine.

considerable outlay required for the dividing-head machines.

Only expert machinists with excellent facilities for precision work should attempt to make a dividing-head machine. The main problem is to ensure that all the moving parts move easily but without looseness. This, coupled with the need for accurate rotational division and angular selection, makes such a project daunting to all but the expert.

The angles of facets are carefully selected for particular gem materials so that maximum brilliance and light refraction is obtained. Standard texts on facetting list the appropriate angles for all gem materials, as well as the patterns for the numerous shapes of facetted stones. Several such reference books will be found in the Bibliography at the end of this book.

Amber   Mohs scale 2.5
This is not really a gem stone, although it is often treated as such. It is a fossilised resin occasionally found on the Norfolk coast, though much of it comes from the Baltic Sea.

Colours: Yellow to reddish brown. Transparent to translucent. Must be dopped with great care since it tends to soften at temperatures in excess of 150°C. If possible, dop with cold adhesive. Amber must be ground and sanded with plenty of water. Polish on damp leather with tin oxide.

Apatite   Mohs scale 5
Colours: Yellow, yellow/green and occasionally blue and purple; transparent or translucent. Sources, Spain and Norway. Dop with care or use a cold dopping adhesive.

Grind with care on a very smooth and accurate wheel and polish on leather with either tin or cerium oxide.

Azurite   Mohs scale 4
As its name implies, azurite is a bright blue material, mostly opaque, though some transparent crystals are occasionally available. Chief source is South-west Africa. Too soft for rings, it is a beautiful stone for pendants and brooches.

It grinds and sands easily on wet wheels, and polishes well on wet, padded leather with tin or cerium oxide.

Beryl   Mohs scale 7.5

Various colours of beryl exist, the best known being emerald (green) and aquamarine (pale blue), but it also occurs in a yellow form (golden beryl), a colourless form (goshenite) and a pink variety (morganite).

The crystals vary from transparent to translucent but frequently contain many flaws and inclusions. The flawed varieties are much cheaper than the perfect crystals and make beautiful cabochons.

There are few problems in cutting and polishing and the stones are insensitive to dopping heat. Polish with cerium oxide on a leather wheel for cabochons and with cerium on a perspex lap for facetting.

Corundum   Mohs scale 9

Best known of the corundums are rubies and sapphires, classically red and blue respectively, but corundum exists in many colours, including orange, green and purple.

As with the beryls, good crystals are extremely expensive, but flawed specimens can be obtained at reasonable cost.

Because of their intense hardness, corundums can only be worked efficiently on diamond wheels. They cause considerable wear on silicon carbide wheels (hardness $9\frac{1}{2}$).

Cabochons can be polished on leather with cerium oxide,

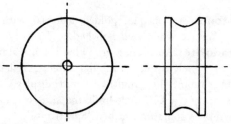

Turned hardwood wheel for sanding or polishing cabochons using diamond compounds.

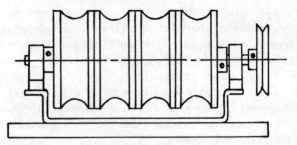

Four hardwood wheels on a single shaft make a complete sanding and polishing unit for cabochon making. Diamond compounds should be 600, 1200, 3000 and 8000 grits.

but a better finish is obtained by polishing on a hardwood wheel with a curved groove in its rim and a paste of fine diamond powder (6400 grit) mixed with grease and gently smoothed into the groove.

Corundums come from Ceylon, Burma, Australia and Montana, U.S.A., but are also produced synthetically (see **Synthetic gems**).

Feldspar   Mohs scale 6
This mineral is found mostly in massive form of many colours, types and names.

Moonstone: An almost clear gem stone of silvery/blue lustre.

Sunstone: An opaque, golden material with a fine, gleaming surface when well polished.

Labradorite: An opaque grey/blue/black material, the surface of which displays 'Schiller effect', reflecting an exquisite shimmering, multi-coloured display. It often contains many cracks which limit the sizes of cabochons. Gem quality is sometimes called 'Spectrolite'.

Amazonite: A green and blue/green material, nearly always opaque.

All feldspars cut and polish easily using the methods outlined previously.

Fluorite   Mohs scale 4

Another rather soft but beautiful stone, fluorite is found in many colours, including green, yellow and blue, and is transparent to translucent. An especially beautiful but disappointingly rare type called 'Blue John' was mined for centuries at Castleton in Derbyshire. This variety is banded white and purple.

Fluorite is rather heat sensitive, so dop with care and treat gently while grinding and sanding. It polishes well on a soft leather wheel with cerium oxide.

Garnet   Mohs scale 7

Many different types are found all over the world. It occurs in round, multi-sided crystals, transparent to translucent.

Garnet was a great favourite of Victorian lapidaries.

Varieties include:

Andradite – green.

Almandine – red to purple.

Grossularite – green, yellow, red.

Pyrope – red.

Spessartite – orange to brown.

The grossularite variety occurs in a massive green form in South Africa and is known as 'Transvaal jade'.

Garnet presents no problems in producing cabochons.

Jadeite   Mohs scale 7

Two minerals are called jade, and the other one, **Nephrite**, is listed separately.

Jade is a remarkably tough, fibrous gem stone which is available in a surprising range of colours apart from green.

It can be obtained in various shades of blue, yellow, purple and red, as well as in white and black.

Always highly prized by the Chinese, there is, surprisingly, no record of any Chinese source. Burma is the major source of jadeite, but other sources – often of inferior grades and colours – exist in many parts of the world.

Jadeite is insensitive to heat and grinds well but is notorious for difficult polishing. Sanding, especially fine sanding, should be prolonged, and the polishing on leather and cerium should be gentle at first but concluded with abrupt pressure. A short period of this will tend to create enough heat to soften the dopping wax, so it will need to be rested between attacks. The fibrous nature of the stone tends to produce an 'orange peel' surface if normal polishing is performed.

Lapis lazuli   Mohs scale 5.5
Translated from the Latin, 'blue stone', lapis is a brilliant blue/purple stone, frequently flecked with white calcite and sometimes sparkling pyrites. The price varies with the number of inclusions. The finest materials come from Afghanistan, Chile and Russia.

Insensitive to heat, the only problem is in polishing, due to variations in hardness of lapis and its inclusions. Fine sanding should be carefully done and then polish rapidly.

Malachite   Mohs scale 4
A massive brilliant green stone often banded with grey or black rings, malachite is ideal for pendant cabochons but too soft for rings. It is an unpleasant stone to cut because it tends to form a heavy sludge, which blocks wheels and sanding discs. However, it cuts easily and quickly – sometimes too quickly – and polishes well on a soft leather wheel with tin oxide.

Nephrite   Mohs scale 6.5

The other jade (see **Jadeite**). Nephrite is slightly softer, but even tougher, than Jadeite and its colour range is less spectacular, being white, yellow, brown or green.

It presents similar polishing problems to jadeite.

Because of its intense toughness, it is a splendid material for carving with diamond tools and points.

Nephrite has a variety of sources, including New Zealand and Wyoming, U.S.A., but tremendous deposits have recently been discovered in British Columbia and Alaska. The difficulty of getting the rough out (20-ton boulders, for instance) will probably keep the price up.

Obsidian   Mohs scale 5.5

Obsidian is volcanic glass, often occurring in huge masses but sometimes found in small nodules. Many such nodules are found in the South-west U.S.A. of a transparent, brownish colour and are known as 'Apache tears'.

It is slightly heat sensitive but polishes well following prolonged fine sanding.

Obsidian shatters if dropped (it is, after all, glass).

Opal   Mohs scale 6

Opal is a colloidal form of silica which contains up to 10 per cent of water. It is mined with great difficulty, from narrow veins and small pockets in rocks.

Opal is found throughout the world but much of it is dull and colourless. The highly coloured 'precious opal' originates mostly in Australia, Mexico and Brazil.

White opal is a white-based material with brilliant colour play.

Black opal has a black or grey base with colour play.

Fire opal is a red or orange, translucent or transparent material.

Jelly opal is nearly transparent with a fairly large colour show.

The colour in opal exists in very thin layers and can easily be ground away. It must, consequently, be ground carefully, and when you reach colour you STOP!

Good-quality opal is extremely expensive. Fine 'rough' can easily cost £100 per ounce, and consequently many stones are cut to irregular cabochon shapes to reveal the maximum area of colour or fire.

Often, colourful material is cut in very thin slices and cemented onto cheaper common opal or 'potch' to build up to usable thickness. These are called doublets. Sometimes, too, a piece of clear quartz – rock crystal – is cemented on top of the opal slice to act as a lens and to protect the softer opal. Such sandwiches are called 'triplets'.

Very thin diamond saws, about 0·010 inch thick, are used to slice precious opal and other costly materials.

Opal is heat sensitive and vibration sensitive, so great care must be taken in dopping and grinding. Gentle sanding and polishing are also advisable.

Phrenite   Mohs scale 6.5
This is a translucent to transparent material of yellow to green colour. It presents no problems when cut and polished as previously described. Chief sources are Scotland and South Africa, and several European countries.

Quartz   Mohs scale 7
Transparent varieties of quartz include:
Amethyst – mauve to deep purple.
Cairngorm – smoky quartz – golden to brown.
Citrine – yellow.
Green quartz – pale green.
Rock crystal – water clear.

Rose quartz – pink. Only rarely transparent, and then rather costly. It is generally translucent with paler streaks.

Rutilated quartz – clear with inclusions of needle-like golden rutile.

Tourmalinated quartz – clear with inclusions of generally black crystals of tourmaline.

Opaque quartzes include:

Adventurine – green or blue/green with a glittering surface.

Prase – dark green, sometimes streaked with pale green.

Cryptocrystalline quartzes are composed of very small crystals and include:

Carnelian – red, orange and white-striped chalcedony.

Chalcedony – pale blue or grey translucent material.

Jasper – massive chalcedony in various colour mixes of brown, green, yellow and red.

Bloodstone – dark green with red spots and flecks.

Agate – layered and banded in a tremendous range of colours and patterns; parts are transparent, translucent and opaque.

Tigers eye – a beautiful gem material from South Africa. It is a curious stone of quartz replacing asbestos. It can be gold/brown, gold/blue or blue. Because of its fibrous construction it possesses chatoyancy, which on a polished cabochon is shown as bands of light that move over the gem. If a cabochon is properly oriented and cut it produces a 'cat's eye', a single bar of light dividing the stone symmetrically.

This great range of quartz materials provides many beautiful and inexpensive gem stones for the lapidary. They rarely produce any problems when cut and polished as previously described.

Various forms are found all over the world and most beaches provide several forms of quartz.

Rhodochrosite   Mohs scale 4
Another rather soft but beautiful material in reddish pink with white bandings, often convoluted to produce beautiful patterns. It requires care in all departments to produce worthwhile gems.

Rhodonite   Mohs scale 6
Often confused with **Rhodochrosite**, but the pink to red colour of this material is nearly always associated with grey or black masses. It has a very coarse grain structure but polishes well, after a lengthy fine sanding, on soft leather and tin oxide.

Sodalite   Mohs scale 6
A medium to dark blue, massive opaque material, generally streaked with white. It works easily and polishes well with cerium oxide. Major source is Canada.

Synthetic gems (See end of this section.)

Topaz   Mohs scale 8
Topaz crystals occur in various colours, including blue, red and green, but the majority range from pale to dark yellow.

The crystals are frequently flawed, which renders them unsuitable for facetting, but they will produce handsome cabochons. Hardness 8 will slow down all processes but presents no problems.

Tourmaline   Mohs scale 7.5

Crystals form long, shield-sectioned rods, but rough material is frequently broken into short lengths.

Colour varies enormously, green and black being the most common, followed by blue, red and pink. Tourmaline sometimes occurs with sections of the crystal in different colours.

The crystals are transparent but often heavily flawed, with dark inclusions.

It requires careful dopping but otherwise presents no problems.

Turquoise   Mohs scale 6

A pale blue to blue/green opaque stone, often with inclusions of other minerals. Careful treatment in all operations is necessary.

Verdite   Mohs scale 3.5

This is a fine material for large cabochons not subject to wear, and for carving. The green and white figure produces interesting patterns. It works easily and polishes well.

Verdite comes from South Africa.

Synthetic gems

Synthetic gems – not to be confused with artificial gems – have been successfully made since the early 1900s. Artificial gems are made from glass or paste, or even from plastic, but synthetic gems are made from the same materials as the natural gem and produced under the same circumstances of heat and pressure that nature used to produce diamonds, rubies, etc.

Generally, the only difference between natural and synthetic gems is the absence of flaws and inclusions in the synthetics, which produces an odd situation. Natural gems with faults and flaws are much more valuable than flawless synthetics, although only a gemmologist with sophisticated equipment could tell positively which was which.

Most industrial diamonds are produced synthetically and experimentation is constantly striving to produce synthetic gem-quality diamonds, but so far the limited output has made them much more expensive than their natural equivalents.

With other gem stones, however, the situation is much more in our favour. A good-coloured natural ruby would cost hundreds of pounds per carat (140th part of an ounce), but a synthetic of equal colour might cost no more than 2 pence per carat in the rough.

The usual range of synthetic stones includes beryls (emeralds, aquamarine, golden beryl and morganite), corundum (rubies and sapphires in all their various colours and shades) and spinels in a wide range of colours.

Synthetics are produced in 'boules', which is a shape of round section rather like a bottle. Often the boules (especially of corundum) are split longitudinally before being sold.

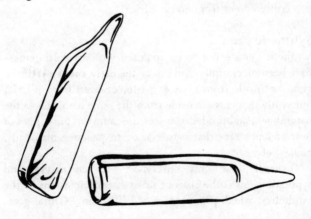

The boules are generally 2 to 3 inches long and weigh up to about 400 carats (about 3 ounces).

Most synthetics are used for facetted stones, but magnificent cabochons can be cut from them. Generally, however, synthetics are produced of the harder gem stones and diamond-cutting equipment is to be preferred – although they can be cut on silicon carbide wheels if you don't object to the slow cutting of the stone and the rapid wear of your wheel.

Several synthetic gem stones are produced which nature never got around to producing itself. Chief among these are strontium titanate, yttrium aluminium garnet (Y.A.G.) and blue quartz.

Strontium titanate is used as a substitute for diamond since it has a high refractive index (a measure of the potential sparkle of the facetted stone). It is much softer than a diamond (Mohs scale 6.5) and is therefore easily distinguished.

Y.A.G. is much harder (Mohs scale 7.5) and is produced in a range of colours as well as the water-clear variety. It produces spectacular facetted gems and beautiful cabochons.

Both these latter materials are more expensive than the synthetic corundums, beryls and spinels.

Blue quartz, a recent product of Russian synthesis, produces beautiful gems but, so far, has not been made available in this country. Small consignments have, however, reached the U.S.A.

11 Setting Up a Workshop

A small lapidary can be set up in a surprisingly compact space, particularly if you purchase one of the combination machines that are available. Such machines, with a trim saw at one end, one or two grinding wheels in the middle and a shaft extension at the other end for fitting sanding and polishing wheels, can be fitted onto a bench 3 feet by 2 feet. With a small cupboard for storing spare wheels, dopping equipment, etc., you are in business.

If you can find a little more space for your workshop, you will find that individual machines are much more convenient and, as has been explained previously, much more amenable to amateur construction.

A long (6 to 8 feet) sturdy bench is to be preferred and its top, preferably made of 1-inch thick blockboard, should be covered with a laminated plastic so that it may be kept spotlessly clean. Wide shelves should be fitted below the bench to store machines not in use and a small cupboard conveniently sited for storing spare wheels, silicon carbide grits, polishing oxides, sanding discs, dopping equipment, drills, etc. A sink with running water should be fitted if at all possible.

Good lighting is essential and can best be provided by a fluorescent tube over the bench, but an additional, adjustable, lamp which can be directed onto particular operations such as lapping, polishing and facetting is a desirable luxury.

With such a workshop, equipped with individual machines, it is possible to set up a single motor which can be quickly coupled to one or two machines. You will need a fairly substantial motor, $\frac{1}{4}$ hp if it will be operating only one machine at a time and $\frac{1}{2}$ hp should you envisage two people working simultaneously on separate machines.

The motor should be mounted on the wall against which the bench is fitted, and it should be placed on a sturdy platform 2 or 3 feet above the bench.

Below the motor, and fixed to the wall about 9 inches

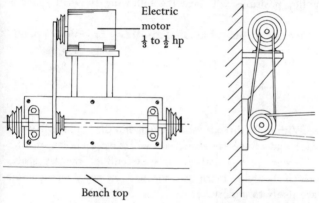

Electric motor $\frac{1}{3}$ to $\frac{1}{2}$ hp

Bench top

Lay shaft arrangement permitting the operation of two machines at one time.

above the bench, is a lay shaft which consists of a long, heavy shaft running in ball bearings. It should have a central pulley connected by a belt to the motor above it, and at each end it should have a triple pulley (3, 4 and 5 inches diameter) to which machines may be coupled. The machines are connected to the pulley, which will give the correct rotation speed, and then the machine is clamped to the bench with G-cramps, making sure that the correct tension is established in the connecting belts.

An additional series of speed adjustments can be provided

by fitting triple pulleys on the motor and the lay shaft. If you do this, pick the same three diameters (3, 4 and 5 inches, for instance) for both the motor and the lay shaft. Ensure that these are fitted so that the 5-inch pulley on the motor is above the 3-inch pulley on the shaft, and vice versa, since this will ensure that the belt will be in correct tension on all of the three positions.

If your motor is 1420 r.p.m. (a standard speed) the three pulley positions will give the following lay shaft speeds:

Motor pulley	Lay shaft pulley	Lay shaft speed
in	in	r.p.m.
3	5	852
4	4	1420
5	3	2365

With these three lay shaft speeds and the triple pulleys on each end of the lay shaft, you will have a choice of nine different speeds available at each end of the lay shaft, which should be more than adequate for any operation you are likely to undertake.

It is as well, particularly if young children are likely to be in the workshop, to fit a simple guard over the belt connecting the motor and the lay shaft.

If you are building your own bench, do ensure that it is high enough for you to work comfortably without bending. Most commercial work benches are constructed to suit quite short people, on the theory that it is easier for tall people to bend over than for short people to stand on a platform. As a fairly tall person with a dodgy back I tend to disagree, and I suggest that you should take a completely selfish attitude when building your own bench.

Ideally, when working at a lapidary machine, your back should be straight and your arms bent at the elbow, with your forearms parallel to the bench top. This means that the bench top should be about 5 inches below your forearms held in this position.

If you permit someone shorter than yourself to work in your lapidary, then a shallow platform can easily be constructed for your guest to stand on.

Other refinements to your lapidary shop will depend on the space available and on your particular interests. There are some machines that cannot easily be coupled up to the lay shaft arrangement, and such machines will need their own built-in motors. These machines include laps, facetting machines, slabbing saws and tumblers, and if you propose using any or all of these machines their operating locations should be considered in your original plans.

A suitable site for a tumbler can usually be found under a bench, and the constant rumbling can be reduced to an acceptable level by standing the tumbler on thick layers of felt or plastic foam and by lining the compartment with one of these materials or expanded polystyrene. Make sure that you leave adequate ventilation, otherwise even a continuous-rating motor might generate too much heat.

Slabbing saws and facetting machines should have permanent sites allocated to them, since such machines are generally too cumbersome to allow frequent moving about. An individual light source is essential, especially for a facetting machine, and should be of the flexible or adjustable type, since the light should be within a few inches of the lap surface and preferably below eye level.

Aim at producing an almost clinical atmosphere by painting bench and walls with white gloss paint, and cover the floor with an easily cleaned surface of linoleum or vinyl floor covering.

Units of small plastic trays are very useful for storing

small pieces of gem material, small slabs and cut stones, while large pieces of rough material can be arranged on shelves. Wide shelves, preferably slightly angled and lipped on the front edge, form very attractive storage displays for sawn slabs. Collect a number of screw-top jars for holding the various grades of silicon carbide grits and polishing oxides, and label them prominently.

12 Making Jewellery

Although the cutting and polishing of gem stones is a satisfying hobby in its own right, there is bound to come a time when you will feel that some of your stones must be turned into jewellery. Even if this does not seem terribly important to you it will occur extremely quickly to the distaff side of your family, who will argue that a jewel in a display cabinet is a jewel wasted. They will argue that there is no finer display surface for a fine gem than a female throat or a female finger or a female ear. They may even be tempted to assert that a masculine shirt-cuff is only sewn onto a shirt so that it may sport a cuff-link, and you will find these arguments progressively more persuasive.

Many of the lapidary supply houses list in their catalogues vast numbers of 'findings', which is the curious word describing the metallic parts of jewellery, the rings, brooches, pendants, ear-rings and cuff-links which only need a gem stone to be fitted for their completion.

These findings are available in many materials, including copper, stainless steel, silver and gold plate as well as sterling silver and 9 kt. gold. Rings, for instance, range in price from a few pence in copper to several pounds in 9 kt. gold, and comparable price ranges will appear for any other type of finding.

You will understand that it is necessary to cut a stone to fit the finding, but since the majority of findings are made to regular sizes as occur in the commercial templates this presents no great problems.

The only snag is that most lapidaries feel, with justifiable pride, that their creations need a ring, for instance, designed to fit the stone, and that the stone should not be made to fit the ring. If you feel like this, you are on the way to becoming a silversmith as well as a lapidary.

This is nothing to be afraid of. Most skills are easily learnt with a little determined effort, and silversmithing is one such skill. The outlay on equipment is quite small and a 2-foot square surface in the corner of the lapidary shop is quite sufficient space.

Silver is a beautifully simple material to work. It is sympathetic to any form of manipulation and is not as expensive as it may sound. It is easily obtainable in sheet, strip, rod or tube of almost infinite sizes and shapes, and a range of chains and fastenings are available to finish off your creations.

Space limitations prevent the inclusion in this book of a section on jewellery-making, but many good books are available, covering all aspects of this subject. Most education authorities run evening classes in the silversmithing aspects of jewellery-making, and even if there is no class available at your local school you will find that the school authorities are often keen to start such classes provided that a minimum number of students can be found.

There also exist in Britain a growing number of lapidary clubs. (A list is included in the appendices.) Many of these clubs have enthusiastic jewellers as well as lapidaries among their members and instruction in the manipulation of silver can frequently be obtained.

Appendices

Lapidary Supply Houses

(Some firms make a charge for their catalogues which is refunded against the first order.)

Complete suppliers
(Machines, materials, rough rock, slabs, findings, etc.)

M. L. Beach,
41 Church Street, Twickenham, Middx.

Craftorama (Wholesale) Co.,
14 Endell Street, London W.C.2.

Gemrocks,
7 Brunswick Shopping Centre, Off Marchmont Street,
London W.C.1.

Gemstones,
44 Walmsley Street, Hull, Yorkshire.

Hirsch Jacobson,
91 Marylebone High Street, London W.1.

Kernowcraft,
44 Lemon Street, Truro, Cornwall.

Machinery/accessories suppliers

Ammonite Limited,
Llandow Industrial Estate,
Cowbridge, Glamorgan, South Wales.
(Importers and distributors of 'Highland Park' –
American – lapidary machinery.)

Benson Bond Ltd.
246 Western Road, Southall, Middx.
(Lapidary grinding wheels, silicon carbide discs.)

Picador Engineering Co. Ltd.,
83 Euston Road, London N.W.1.
(Belts, pulleys, shafts, bearings, grinding wheels.)

Proops Brothers,
52 Tottenham Court Road, London W.1.
(Small 'continuous-rated' electric motors
and other equipment.)

Strand Glass Co.,
79 High Street, Brentford, Middx.
(Fibreglass and resin.)

K. R. Whiston,
New Mills, Stockport, Cheshire.
(Picador shafts, bearings, pulleys and belts, and a
varied selection of other constructional materials.)

Whithear Lapidary Co.,
35 Ballards Lane, London N.3.
(Lapidary machines and accessories.)

Johnson-Mathey Metals Ltd.,
73 Hatton Garden, London E.C.1.
(Silver, gold, solders, fluxes.)

Books and Periodicals

Gem Cutting by John Sinkankas
Published by Van Nostrand Reinhold £4.15

Gem Stones by G. F. H. Smith
Published by Methuen £3.50

Collecting Rocks and Fossils by Justin B. Delair
Published by Batsford £1.25

Gem Craft by L. Quick and H. Leiper
Published by Pitman £3.00

Minerals and Rocks in Colour by J. F. Kircaldy
Published by Blandford £1.50

The Design and Creation of Jewelry by Robert von Neumann
Published by Pitman £3.00

Handwrought Jewelry by Lois B. Frank
Published by McKnight and McKnight £4.50

Gems – The British Lapidary Magazine
Published by Lapidary Publications,
20 Ludgate Hill, London E.C.4. Bi-monthly. 17 p per copy

Lapidary Journal
Published by Lapidary Journal Inc.,
P.O. Box 2369, San Diego, California, U.S.A.
Subscription rates – $6.25 per year (thirteen issues)
$12.00 for two years (international money order)

Rock and Gem

Published by Behn-Miller Publishers Inc.,
16250 Ventura Blvd., Encino, California 91316.
Six issues for $5.00 (bi-monthly)

Clubs and Societies in Britain

Scottish Clubs

Pentland Lapidary Society,
12 Kirkgate, Currie, Midlothian.

Golspie Lapidary Club,
The Wee Shop, Golspie, Sutherland.

West of Scotland Mineral & Lapidary Society,
82 Dumbreck Road, Glasgow S.1.

Borders Lapidary Club,
47 Albert Place, Galashiels, Selkirkshire.

Longniddry Lapidary Society,
15 Main Street, Longniddry, East Lothian.

Black Isle Lapidary Club,
Sec., J. L. Alexander,
'Asgarth', North Kessock, Ross-shire.

Sutherland Rockhounds,
Wester Lonemore, Dornach, Sutherland.

Scottish Mineral & Lapidary Club,
Sec., Adam Montgomery,
22B St. Giles Street, Edinburgh 1.

Kirkaldy Mineral & Lapidary Club,
73 Dinnikier Road, Kirkcaldy, Fife.

Falkirk Lapidary Club,
Sec., Mrs. A. Archibald,
72 Slamannan Road, Falkirk.

Ancrum Lapidary Club,
Ancrum Activities Centre,
10 Ancrum Road, Dundee DD2 2HZ.

North England Clubs

Kingston Lapidary Society,
219 Summergangs Road, Hull HU8 8LD.

Teeside Lapidary Society,
Sec., Mrs. M. Carter,
65 Staindrop Drive, Acklam, Middlesbrough.

Harrogate & District Geology and Lapidary Society,
Sec., Mrs. D. M. Proctor,
71 Wetherby Road, Harrogate.

Fylde Mineral & Lapidary Society,
c/o Mr. McEwan,
Lytham St. Anne's College of Further Education,
St. Anne's on Sea, Lancs.

Stanley Rockhound Club,
Sec., C. P. Wilkinson,
24 Cecil Street, East Stanley, Stanley, Co. Durham.

The Peak District Rock & Mineral Society,
c/o Mr. R. Hill,
The Tideswell Youth Centre, Tideswell, Derby.

The Danum Lapidary Society,
Sec., Mrs. P. Birkett,
39 St. Augustines Road, Bessacarr, Doncaster.

Whitehaven and District Mineral & Lapidary Society,
Sec., E. Halliday,
110 Tomlin Avenue, Mirehouse, Whitehaven.

The Leeds Lapidary Society,
Sec., Miss J. Adamson,
2 Earlswood Avenue, Leeds LS8 2BR.

Warrington Mineral & Lapidary Society,
Sec., M. J. Jeffrey,
28 Thelwall New Road, Thelwall, Warrington, Lancs.

Huddersfield Mineralogical Society,
Sec., I. R. Blezard,
25 Branch Street, Paddock, Huddersfield HD1 4JL.

Sheffield Amateur Geological & Lapidary Society,
Sec., D. Elliston,
5 Hutcliffe Wood Road, Sheffield S8 OEX.

Midlands Clubs

The North West Lapidary Society,
Sec., R. I. Willis,
79 Dean Drive, Wilmslow, Cheshire.

West Midlands Gem & Mineral Society,
Sec., C. C. Berthelsen,
71 Lion Fields Avenue, Allesley, Coventry.

I.C.I. Stowmarket Lapidary Club,
Chairman, D. Hall,
14 Wayside Close, Stowmarket, Suffolk.

Cheltenham Mineral & Geological Society,
Sec., R. R. Dennis,
2 Westcote Road, Tuffley, Gloucester.

Cambridge Lapidary Club,
Sec., J. Whitehead,
93 Queen Edith's Way, Cambridge.

London Clubs

The Amateur Geological Society,
Hampstead Garden Suburb Institute,
Central Square, London N.W.11.

The Essex Rock & Mineral Society,
Emerson Park Social Centre, Slewins Lane, Hornchurch.

Liaison Committee of London and
    Home Counties Geological Societies,
Sec., H. Lister,
176 Wanstead Park Road, Ilford, Essex.

S.E. England Clubs

North Surrey Lapidary Society,
Sec., S. Wilding,
28 The Causeway, Carshalton, Surrey.

The Farnham Geological Society,
Sec., Mrs. P. Crosby,
The Pond Cottage, Pond Lane, Churt, Surrey.

Thanet Mineral & Lapidary Society,
Sec., F.C. Hobbs,
5 Masons Rise, Broadstairs, Kent.

West Surrey Lapidary Society,
Sec., Mrs. M. A. Barnett,
'Elm Croft', Lower Froyle, Alton, Hants.

Dartford Lapidary Society,
Sec., Miss M. E. Elliott,
45A Elmdene Road, Plumstead, London S.E.18.

Sussex Mineral & Lapidary Society,
Sec., K. S. Fitch,
Treyarnon, 17 Dukes Road, Lindfield, Sussex.

S.W. England Clubs

Wessex Lapidary Society,
Sec., Mrs. A. Eastman,
3 Brookfield Road, Fair Oak, Eastleigh, Hants SO5 7EX.

Bath & District Lapidary Society,
Sec., Mrs. E. Parmenter,
10 Pulteney Street, Bath.

Plymouth Mineral & Mining Club,
Chairman, O. A. Baker,
36 Ponsonby Road, Milehouse, Plymouth, Devon.

Bristol & District Lapidary Society,
Sec., Mrs. K. Shortman,
10 Grove Park, Redland, Bristol BS6 6PP.

Southampton Lapidary Society,
Sec., J. Greaves,
7 Laburnum Grove, Eastleigh, Hants.

The Mid-Cornwall Rocks & Minerals Club,
Chairman, Peter Hodkinson,
91 Queens Crescent, Bodmin, Cornwall.

Dorset Mineral and Lapidary Club,
Sec., Mrs. M. Snell,
Bowdens, Broad Oak, Sturminster, Newton, Dorset.

New Forest & Christchurch District
    Mineral & Lapidary Society,
Sec., Miss E. Bailey,
7 Litchford Road, New Milton, Hants.

Irish Club

The Irish Lapidary Society,
Sec., Edith Hammond,
Grafton Court, Grafton Street, Dublin 2.

Chart 1 Motor pulley/machine pulley size
Based on a motor speed of 1420 r.p.m.

Motor pulley size (dia./in)	Machine pulley size (diameter in inches)											
	$1\frac{1}{2}$	$1\frac{3}{4}$	2	$2\frac{1}{2}$	3	$3\frac{1}{2}$	4	5	6	7	8	9
$1\frac{1}{2}$	1420	1220	1065	850	710	610	530	425	355	300	265	235
$1\frac{3}{4}$	1660	1420	1250	995	825	710	620	500	420	355	310	275
2	1890	1625	1420	1135	950	810	710	570	470	405	355	320
$2\frac{1}{2}$	2265	2000	1775	1420	1200	1000	860	710	590	510	440	400
3	2840	2435	2130	1700	1420	1200	1050	850	710	610	530	470
$3\frac{1}{2}$	3200	2840	2485	2000	1660	1420	1245	1050	830	710	620	550
4	3785	3250	2840	2270	1890	1620	1420	1140	950	810	710	630
$4\frac{1}{2}$	4260	3650	3200	2560	2130	1830	1600	1280	1065	910	800	710
5	4730	4060	3550	2840	2365	2030	1775	1420	1185	1015	880	785

Example

Your motor has a 4-inch pulley and you want a grinder to run at approximately 2300 r.p.m. Look along the horizontal line level with 4-inch motor pulley and you will see that a $2\frac{1}{2}$-inch machine pulley will give you 2270 r.p.m.

Chart 2 **Peripheral speed in surface feet per minute (s.f.p.m.) to machine shaft speed in r.p.m. for various wheel or saw diameters**

Peripheral speeds in surface feet per minute (s.f.p.m.)

Wheel or saw (dia./in)	1000	1500	2000	2500	3000	3500	4000	4500	5000
4	950	1425	1900	2375	2850	3325	3800	4275	4750
5	795	1200	1590	1990	2385	2790	3180	3580	3980
6	635	955	1275	1590	1900	2230	2500	2865	3200
7	545	820	1090	1275	1635	1810	2180	2365	2725
8	475	710	950	1185	1430	1666	1900	2135	2400
9	420	630	840	1050	1260	1470	1680	1890	2100
10	380	570	760	950	1150	1330	1530	1710	1900

Example

You wish to operate an 8-inch diameter saw at 3000 s.f.p.m. Look along the 8 inches row and down the 3000 column. They meet at 1430 and this is the required machine shaft speed in r.p.m.